Sex Is Dead

and Other Postmortems

Sex Is Dead

AND OTHER
POSTMORTEMS

Earl H. Brill

THE SEABURY PRESS

NEW YORK

TO LESLEY, GRACE, AND KENNETH

who will shortly inherit this culture of ours

Preface

TO A NUMBER of people who have helped to make this book possible, I should like to express my heartfelt thanks. John C. Goodbody and Arthur R. Buckley of Seabury Press have been most helpful and encouraging. My wife, Ruth, read most of the manuscript and offered more than the usual number of useful wifely criticisms. My students and colleagues at the American University have, at one time or other, listened to me expound the ideas here set forth. Their criticisms and corrections have been valuable, though I would not hold them responsible for any faults in the finished product.

Grateful acknowledgment is also made to the editors of *The Christian Century* for permission to republish here the article "Sex Is Dead!" from the August 3, 1966, issue.

E.H.B.

Contents

Sex Is Dead

and Other Postmortems

1

Sex Is Dead

SEX is dead. Nobody seems to have noticed its passing, what with the distraction caused by recent reports of the death of God, the death of Self, the death of the City, the death of Tragedy, and all the other cultural obituaries of the past few years. Yet it is a fact: sex is dead and we must begin to learn how to live in a world in which that is an incontrovertible fact.

There are numerous signs of the death of sex, particularly on the college campuses. In recent years there has been a marked decline in the traditional preoccupation of college students with sex. Sex used to be the favorite topic of campus discussions, the chief bone of contention between students and administrators. But in the past decade its place has been usurped: first by the civil rights movement, then by the student "freedom movement," the drive for participatory democracy on the campus. This year, war—or, rather, antiwar— seems to be the chief topic on the campus agenda. In any case, sex as a central concern of the "college student" has been running a poor third at best.

Look, for example, at the way college girls dress. The short, short skirt made the springtime campus blossom into a veritable skin show (at least by the standards of my own youth). You might suppose that this indicates an increasing sex consciousness, but you would be quite mistaken: it means the very opposite.

For, in fact, the creeping nudity of female fashions goes quite unnoticed by the young men. To most of them it doesn't occur to give a second look at a well turned thigh. Not so with their elders. I have been conducting a little poll among my colleagues, and it seems that they (let's be honest—*we*) are the overage beneficiaries of the new landscape. We were brought up in the sexual age, and we still keep the faith. But the young men fail to appreciate the aesthetic delights of their environment. It is all quite meaningless to them because sex is dead.

"But ah," you say, "every spring, every fall, whenever the air is balmy and wherever the grass is soft, the campus boys and girls pair off for the same old sensuous wrestling matches. Every year, in fact, the lovers seem to get bolder and bolder." You are quite right, of course. A senior administrator of my acquaintance, a few years ago, was forced to suspend a young man who had been observed studying female anatomy, apparently by the Braille system, on the grass just in front of the administration building. "I wasn't trying to interfere with his love life," the dean explained. "I just got tired of intruding into this seduction scene every time I turned toward my window."

Yet a curious paradox emerges upon inspection of the apparent increase in such uninhibited behavior. There was a time when the campus idol and the campus sweetheart—the aggressive and the lovely, the healthy and the attractive—were the lovers-on-the-lawn. Lately, though, it is rather the homely and the odd who do the biological wrestling: scrawny, pimply-faced boys—the kind Holden Caulfield would have called "hard-up guys"—and fat and frowsy girls who need have no fear of walking across the campus alone at midnight. They create a picture not of two healthy, lusty animals reveling in their sexuality and their freedom, but of two scared and unhappy young people leaning on each other, compulsively clawing at each other as if to say to themselves, to each other and to the world: "See! We know the game! We can play, too." The rituals go on, but they have lost any conviction because sex is dead.

It doesn't take a profound social analyst to demonstrate the basic asexuality of the world of fashion. Flip through *Vogue* or even the fashion pages of your local newspaper, and you will see sample after sample of square, shapeless angular dresses that resolutely deny that they cover warm, soft, curvy female flesh. Look at the with-it haircuts that make women appear ascetic and severe and the men look wan and languid. It's not enough to counter that fashion merely reflects the commercial demand for rapid and dramatic change that will sell new wardrobes every year. The question is, Why should this kind of fashion become the rage at this point in our history? The answer? Sex is dead.

Certainly pop music and the style of dancing that goes with it testify to the death of sex. Whatever else you say about the insistent beat, the strident voices, the primitive tonal patterns, you cannot contend that they add up to sexy music. It is intense music, to be sure, but for all its vigor it is a music without real passion. It may arouse the adrenalin but not the libido.

As numerous observers have pointed out, pop music accompanies a style of dancing that is just as astringent as the music. The movements, like the women's fashions in *Vogue*, are all angles—jerks and twists. This dancing is athletic but hardly suggestive. It keeps people apart rather than wrapping them up in each other. A cartoon many years ago showed a proper Englishman watching an American dance floor where one of the particularly erotic routines of the day was being performed. The visitor was saying: "And after this, I presume they get married?" You can't imagine a foreigner responding in quite that way even to the most enthusiastic performance of the discotheque set.

Perhaps the most convincing illustration of the death of sex comes out of an insight of Marshall McLuhan, who has been teaching us new ways to look at our environment. McLuhan, speaking of the relationship of technology to culture, points out that every new technology creates a new environment which translates the old environment into an art form. Once the old environment no longer surrounds us totally, it becomes visible. That's why we put Model-T Fords into museums.

Now just stretch this observation over a wider area of culture and apply it to sex. When sex was truly a total preoccupation, our major concern was to become free so that we could express ourselves sexually. We tried to fight repressions, inhibitions, and conventional restrictions.

But in recent years, sex has become an art form. We buy quantities of how-to-do-it books; we construct models of Adequate Sexual Behavior and try desperately to conform to the images we have constructed. The development of sex as art form probably reached its culmination with the recent publication of *The Human Sexual Response*, by William H. Masters and Virginia E. Johnson, which describes in meticulous detail how the sexual act is carried out, how the body temperature changes, the pulse rate increases, the muscles tense. Imaginative writers have frequently described the accompaniment to heterosexual genital activity with such phrases as "her pulses quickened" or "he was sweating like a stallion." Now we are given chapter and verse, number and sequence. Now, perhaps, we can construct from the data the Perfect Sex Act and get it preserved for all time in silver at the National Bureau of Standards. Or perhaps, if it is to be generally accepted as a true art form, the model ought to be exhibited in the Museum of Modern Art.

I consider the case for the death of sex as proved, though, of course, I concede that there is still a lot of sex around. Babies are born every day, not all of them conceived by artificial insemination. People still claim to fall in love, and young men and women still take sexual problems to their pastors. Plays and novels are still expected to include a predictable amount of good clean sex. Movie ads continue to feature busty chicks in various stages of dishabille, whether or not the film delivers what it promises. Indeed, much of today's advertising is still predicated on the question that Philip Wylie (remember him?) ascribed to it years ago: "Madam, are you a good lay?" If sex is dead, it is a very lively corpse, as the saying goes.

This line of argument might be more convincing had it not already been effectively answered in another context: by the death-of-God theologians. How can God be dead when there is so much activity in the churches? Easy. Church activity is merely a substitute for an absent God. What we see is not deep religion but shallow religiosity. Religiosity is not faith but only the continuation of a pattern of activity that once, perhaps, had significance, but is now merely formal and conventional, routine observance on the part of people who just haven't yet heard that God is dead.

The same with sex. What seems to flourish is only a set of activities that once meant the presence of sex but does so no longer. We might call it "sexiosity": the perpetuation of routine sexual activities which lack conviction and meaning. Sexiosity is characteristic of people out of another era, people who are not in the know, people who have not heard that sex is dead.

Note the way that sex is normally used in the novel, in the theater, in the movies today. Entertainment sexiosity is neither lusty nor joyful. It is a Big Problem. It gets out of hand. It makes people unhappy. Looking back through the years, you find that every new breakthrough in the treatment of sex in literature or drama has soon produced boredom and indifference. Hence, writers have had to resort to more and more exotic forms of sex to keep interest alive. Fornication gave way to adultery, which was followed in quick succession by homosexuality, incest, rape and sado-masochism. And once Tennessee Williams had treated us to the spectacle of cannibalism, it was pretty hard to find a topper.

What does all this prove? I ask you. If sex were alive and vital, wouldn't the portrayal of ordinary, normal, healthy sexuality be attractive enough to keep people coming back for more without the need to probe constantly into increasingly esoteric perversions? Doesn't the need to range so far afield in the search for kicks indicate that there's nothing there, at the center of concern? Doesn't it suggest that our so-called preoccupation with sex is a great big myth? I think it does.

Well then, what about *Playboy*, the bible of sex culture? Sells pretty well, doesn't it? What about those pages and pages of big, bare-breasted beauties in glorious living color? Are the boys buying *Playboy* for the interviews?

Good question, but too easy, really. *Playboy* is simply the house organ of the fundamentalists of sexiosity. It shouts, "Sex is alive! It is! It is!" It shouts so loud that you wonder whether it believes itself. Hugh Hefner figures as the Billy Graham of sexiosity. He is trying to preserve the remnants of an irrelevant and dying faith. He won't succeed, of course, but meantime there is a buck to be made. People whose faith has been shaken are well known to be generous in rewarding the master who makes an energetic attempt to support them in what they want to believe.

Remember the old *Esquire* magazine, the *Playboy* of a generation ago? *Esquire* was hairy enough to get into trouble with the post-office department during the Truman Administration. Then it decided to acquire class. It hired a few first-rate writers and journalists to do its material, and what happened? Within a few years, people were reading the articles instead of looking at the pictures. Today you can hardly find a decent filthy picture in the whole magazine. I predict that *Playboy* will follow the same route. Already people are actually beginning to read some of the material that Hefner puts in for padding. Of course, Hefner won't take the girls out of the pages of *Playboy*; he's too old. But the next generation will. By the time the present college generation has reached the age of ancients like Hefner and me, the death of sex will be an acknowledged fact, and no magazine editor in his right mind will waste money on models posing in the buff. That kind of thing won't sell —except, of course, to a handful of diehard sexiosity fundamentalists.

What does it mean for us to recognize that sex is dead? What difference will it make? I confess I don't know. I suspect that as we demythologize sex, we will find that we have lost a lot of our anxiety. Maybe then parents and preachers will come to realize that they have been fighting a shadow. Maybe young people will discover the ephemeral nature of the will-o'-the-wisp they have been taught to pursue.

In the meantime, perhaps we ought to explore the forces that led to the development of sex culture, so that we might understand how we ever got into this situation in the first place.

2

Sex Culture in
Its Last Throes

Most people tend to view sex as a biological matter or as a psychological phenomenon. If they are particularly conscientious, they may see it as a moral issue or even as a theological concern. Sex is all of these, of course, but it is also a cultural fact. Our views and attitudes about sex are shaped not only by our biology and our psychology but by our culture.

Man's culture, the anthropologists tell us, gives him his attitudes and values. It shapes the way he looks at issues, and it even decides for him which issues he will regard as worth worrying about. Our own culture has largely determined the way we think about sex. It teaches us most of what we know about sex, including a lot of things that are not so.

We all "know" that sex is the most important drive in human personality. It is overwhelming and irresistible. Anything that goes wrong with anyone's personality is likely to be related in some way to sex. In our society, sexual adjustment is the thing to be most greatly desired —the modern equivalent of the beatific vision.

This may all be true, but if so, it is not because of the fundamental structure of human personality. The cause is more likely to be rooted in our culture than in our biology. If the anthropologists are right about cultural conditioning, then perhaps we ought to regard with some skepticism any statement that interprets man's present condition in absolute terms. Certainly we can question the tendency to absolutize the sex drive.

Our belief in the centrality of sex comes from the theories of Sigmund Freud—as they have been popularly understood and interpreted. It might be useful to ask why Freud viewed sexuality as being so important. No doubt it was because his clinical experience forced the conclusion upon him. Many of his patients were people whose personality disorders were related to sexual repressions. But let it not be forgotten that Freud's work took shape in Vienna at the end of the nineteenth century. That fact alone explains some things.

The latter part of the nineteenth century represents a very peculiar period in the history of Western culture. It was the time of triumph of bourgeois values and morals, which are typified by Queen Victoria, who gave her name to the era. Of course, the Queen did not bring the age about; she was merely its most notable examplar. Like the Queen herself, the Victorian period was an age of respectable morality. It was cool and polite on the outside. But its surface calm was belied by the turbulence and passion that lay just beneath. The sharp cleavages in the culture were matched by sharp cleavages in people. It was, overwhelmingly, an age of neurosis.

Repression was a characteristic of this tight little world. Respectable Victorians refused to admit the existence of anything considered coarse or vulgar. They invented scores of euphemisms to describe the physical functions. Chamber pots and water closets—themselves euphemisms—were banned from polite conversation. People no longer died, they "passed away." Women did not get pregnant. They were "in the family way" if married, or, if not, they were "in trouble."

Naturally this repressive attitude extended into the area of sex. Indeed, most of the repressions were probably related to sex. Sex was a dirty animal function. Though married people were required to engage in a certain amount of sexual activity, they were expected to endure it, not enjoy it.

Modern observers tend to equate Victorian society with the whole of Western culture. Victorian prudery becomes equated with "traditional Christian sexual mores." The church frequently comes under heavy censure for having a rigid and repressive attitude toward sex, though such a charge is rather difficult to support from the historical record.

To be sure some Christian writers in every age have taken a dim view of human sexual practices. It is also true that in Western culture, sex was always hedged about with safeguards because the guardians of morality knew and feared its power. But, although the Christian ages treated sex with respect, they did not normally place it in the center of morality.

Christian moralists have traditionally maintained high standards for sexual behavior. Fornication and adultery have always been considered sinful. Rape and incest were punishable offenses. But the church's attitude toward sex was not especially repressive. Sex was a fact of life. Everyone knew about it. Bawdy humor was commonplace back in the Middle Ages. The four-letter Anglo-Saxon words that described sexual and other physical functions were part of the common speech. You even heard them from the pulpit.

The Christian ages were also realistic about human behavior. Even the stern, judgmental Puritans were not especially severe in their treatment of sexual offenders. In Puritan New England, a couple guilty of fornication were required to confess their sin—before the whole congregation in the earlier days—and then they were forgiven and the matter was dropped. Censure and excommunciation were reserved for offenders who refused to confess. They were punished for their obstinance, not for their sexual behavior. Moreover, the discipline of the Puritan community laid no particular stress on sexual morality. That is, they did not have our curious view that if you use the word "morals," you really mean sex. They had other sins to contend with—sins like blasphemy and contumacy—sins that we've never heard of.

This attitude underwent a vast change in the Victorian era. Bawdiness was considered low and vulgar and was relegated to the segregated masculine society. Sex was referred to, if at all, in those polite circumlocutions so characteristic of the age. Not only was sexual activity considered disgusting, but even erotic thoughts and feelings were frowned upon. Nice girls didn't think about such things. Those who did were told to put the dirty thoughts out of their minds. If a girl had feelings that were considered inappropriate, those, too, had to be denied. Of course, all such exiled thoughts and feelings only went underground to make their assaults upon the personality in the form of dreams and neuroses.

This was the world in which Freud lived and worked. He took the lid off the unconscious and discovered the unholy brew that was bubbling up inside. He concluded that the only way man could keep from blowing up was to release the pent-up tensions by making conscious what was in the unconscious. This is what psychoanalysis is supposed to do.

In his later years, Freud thought more about the wider implications of his discoveries. He decided that repression is inevitable if men are to live in civilization. Man, he concluded, will always be torn between his desires and the demands of civilized life. Freud saw no way out of the dilemma. He concluded, reluctantly, that civilization is worth the price and that man would just have to learn to live with his discontents.

In the cultural climate of Freud's Vienna—or New York, for that matter—his conclusion is undoubtedly warranted. But culture itself changes. It has changed considerably since Freud's time. His own work has had much to do with bringing about the change.

For one thing, Freud's discovery of the relationship of sexuality to repression and neurosis brought the subject of sex out into the open. People started talking about it again. Victorian prissiness, though it lingers on, received its death blow. Sexual practices became freer.

Kissing in public was no longer considered promiscuous. Women's clothing styles reflected their new sexual freedom. Women were no longer required to deny their sexuality—they could emphasize it. Plays and novels with sexual themes were permitted and approved, where once they had to be read in secret. Sex moved back into the culture, and it quickly occupied the very center of things.

It is not too hard to understand why that should have happened. An appetite that is long denied expression will take its vengeance once it is released. A man who has been half-starved all his life will very likely gorge himself with food if he comes suddenly into money. A young person who has been brought up to believe that drinking liquor is evil is very likely to hit the bottle hard once he moves into a society in which drinking is not only approved but encouraged.

This is pretty much what happened to us in the Great Sexual Revolution. Now that we could once more talk about sex, it soon began to seem, as C. S. Lewis once pointed out, that we could talk of nothing else. New freedom in the public display of affection went further every year. Clothing continued to assert woman's freedom until she was left with very little to hide. From the floor-length gown to the bikini—that describes the movement of woman's sexual freedom. Literature progressed to the point at which every sexual practice and malpractice had been described with infinite and painstaking attention to the minutest detail. Advertising exploited the undraped female form to the point of saturation.

Freud found a culture which had dammed up the human sex drive behind a great wall of repression. He made a few cracks in the wall and was astonished at the force of the torrent that poured out. He concluded that here, indeed, was the great reservoir of energy which drives human personality.

Since Freud's time that wall of repression has received blow after blow until, by now, it is almost totally demolished in the more sophisticated areas of our society. The immediate result of that demolition was a vast flood, such as we might expect when any dam breaks. Sex has spilled out all over us, threatening to submerge us all. It has dominated drama, literature, movies, clothing style, advertising, morality, and ordinary conversation.

Most of us living in the past thirty years have assumed that this condition is permanent and inevitable. But if the analogy of the broken dam is an accurate one, then we might conclude that the flood conditions are only temporary. As time goes on, repression will become a mere survival, and sexuality will take its normal place in life. Though still operative, it will be subordinate to other forces, other motives, other interests.

Freud himself saw this coming. His own theory of sexuality is much more general and comprehensive than is our common use of the term. He meant any pursuit of pleasure connected with the body. Adult sexuality, which in our culture is interpreted purely as genital activity, is for Freud a narrow limitation of the possibilities of sexual life. When we broke down the dam of repression, the sexual activity that was released was all genital. This is what now appears to be subsiding. As it continues to subside, we will reach the point at which we will begin to see that coitus is not the obvious culmination of man's search for pleasurable activity. It certainly is one culmination, but there are others. Our sense of taste is largely underdeveloped. We have never

even begun to exploit the sensual pleasures associated
with the sense of smell. I would put my money on the
arts as providing the most likely opportunity for
pleasurable stimulation. In any case, we still have a lot to
learn about pleasure.

What complicates the picture for us is the survival of
sex culture, which surrounds us with an ideology that
most of us take for granted. This ideology views sex
simply as orgasm. It preaches the omnipotence of
genital desire. It proclaims the joys of sexual freedom
conceived in these narrow terms, and it moralizes
sternly about the dangers resulting from failure to seize
every opportunity for "free sexual expression." It has
produced an inverted Puritanism in which sexual adjustment is the new standard and anyone who fails to conform to the pattern is put to shame.

In other words, as the floods subside a whole army
of opportunists who have been making their living off
the flood waters have turned to the pumps to keep the
water at a high level through artificial means. They minister to the remnants of repression through various
subtle variants of pornography: the bare bosom in the
movie ad; the tiresomely "daring" film that "tells all
for the first time"; the continuing crusade for sexual
freedom, which usually means the demand for social approval of perversion and pornography.

It's about time we began to encourage people to chal-
lenge the shaky assumptions of sex culture. Sex is not
the sole ruling passion of the world—except for people
who choose to make it so. Sex culture is losing its grip,
and anything that we can do to help the process along is
all to the good. Our culture will be a lot healthier when
businessmen find they can no longer exploit people's

sexual desires and longings in order to sell them things, when young people find more important things to worry about than the state of their sex lives. Only when that day finally comes will we begin to catch a wider vision of what sexuality really means.

I am not calling for a new repression. After all, pruriency and pornography stem from the same cultural milieu. I am merely asking that we stop overdoing the whole sexual routine. The flood is over, and it is time we acknowledge the fact. When we see our sexual problems in perspective, we will be able to do something about them. So long as we assume that we are handling dynamite, we are afraid to even try.

So let's not take the stuffy pretensions of sex culture too seriously. People are already finding that the fulfillment of basic human desires is a lot more complicated than getting into bed with somebody. As we look around at the whole range of possible joys and satisfactions, we can begin to view sex as it really is and put it where it really belongs. And as we do, we will come to see that there is less to this problem than meets the eye.

3

Is Marriage Dying, Too?

IF SEX is dead, can marriage long survive? After all, since time immemorial, reluctant males have been lured into marriage through the instrumentality of plain, old-fashioned sex. Now what are we going to do? What sense will we be able to make of St. Paul's left-handed justification for marriage—". . . for it is better to marry than to burn"—in an age in which no one is burning?

Our society has traditionally viewed marriage as the way to legitimize sexual activity. Of course, there is something to that. Christian pastors have for years been telling prospective brides and grooms that marriage provides the only possible context for genuinely free love. That is, only a person who enjoys the total security offered by the marriage vows can afford to express himself sexually without fear of being rejected by the partner.

To be sure, that view has been somewhat shaken by the easy accessibility of divorce. If divorce is cheap and convenient, then the stability of marriage may become eroded to the point where marriage partners have hardly any real security in their relationship. But on the other hand, even today there are very few husbands or wives who ever think of divorce as a possible threat to their own marriage. When you begin thinking that way, you're in trouble already.

We do have curious ideas about the relationship of sex to marriage. Unmarried people like to point out that in any discussion of sexual morality, the conversation is always dominated by the question of premarital chastity. Apparently once you're married, there are no more problems, certainly no more moral issues.

That's a fair criticism. You don't hear nearly enough about the moral issues involved in marriage. Yet psychiatrists and pastoral counselors frequently observe that most marital problems have a sexual component. Anxiety, sexual maladjustment, inadequacy, and exploitation are prevalent in marriage. Maybe that's why middle-aged adults like to dwell upon the immoralities of unmarried youth.

Our attitude toward marriage is complicated by the way we pile up our expectations about it. Marriage is supposed to be the cure for everything from boredom to psychosis. My hair curls whenever I hear someone refer to some young person whose frailties and inadequacies stick out all over, suggesting that what he (she) really needs is a good wife (husband). You wonder what people have against the poor partner who is going to be saddled with the task of shepherding the little neurotic through life.

Then, too, the marriage-preparation industry seems to be geared to programming a peculiarly specious kind of married happiness. Are you both well-rounded people? Do you share common interests? Why not learn to ski together? Check this list and see if you like the same things. If not, you may be a poor marriage risk.

If this is what marriage compatibility really means, then the people who have been matching up prospective couples via the computer may be on the right track. If a list of external similarities is the best guarantee for a happy marriage, then the computer is probably as good a judge of the chances as is any frail human being.

The problem with our commendable expectations about marriage is that we can seldom live up to them. Marriage seldom makes new people out of old ones, or healthy ones out of sick ones. Sexual adjustment, about which people write volumes of turgid prose, is apparently pretty rare. Most people go through life bumbling toward something which they can label as satisfactory. Until we discovered sex, nobody expected much else, so no one was too disappointed. Now we find ourselves free from traditional repressions but bound by a new kind of inverse puritanism in which sexual morality in marriage is equated with some mysterious ingredient called adjustment, which most people can't produce. And the result? Frustration, despair, and often a panicky search for new partners.

The most curious aspect of our attitude toward marriage is our unspoken assumption that every normal red-blooded adult ought to indulge in it. This is certainly a new idea. The Middle Ages didn't hold with it. But, of course, we have the answer to that one. The Middle Ages were dark ages. They denied the goodness of man's natural appetites. They confined men and women unnaturally in convents and monasteries. These had to be places of perversion and secret sinfulness. They had to be, because all men naturally engage in sexual activity, and marriage is their normal estate.

So we are unambiguously *for* marriage—for everybody. Look at the way we treat single people in our own social circles. First we try to match up our single friends. We invite eligible males to dinner to meet our single female friends, and then we sit back to see what will happen. When chemistry has done its work, and we hear that a pair of them are engaged to each other, we applaud ourselves for a good job done.

There are always those, both male and female, who escape the tender trap. We keep trying, but they insist on preserving their single blessedness. Finally we give up and consign them to a category: confirmed bachelor; old maid. As we begin to lose hope, we also lose touch. Finally we're reduced to having them in for dinner occasionally to round out a party. We relegate them to the edges of our married society and trot them out only when we need their peculiar status for reasons of our own.

So the pressures toward marriage are a strange combination of sex and sociability. Both seem a little pointless, because marriage is much more than either of them. From now on, however, we may begin to see less pressure for marriage. At least, the young people may begin putting off the date until they are really sure they want to do it. If we are lucky, this new generation may show a more ready acceptance of the unmarried state, so that the second pressure for marriage may someday go the way of the first.

Then what will happen? Will marriage disappear? Will we witness the end of family life? Will we see a massive decline in the population?

I doubt that any of these things will happen, but I think we will see real changes in marriage: in the way we look at it and in the way we practice it.

For one thing, we can expect that marriage will no longer be regarded—as it now is, especially by girls—as a success symbol. Already there is considerable evidence of disenchantment with this aspect of marriage.

Back in the nineteen-twenties, I am told, a college girl looked forward to a useful and satisfying career if she were with it at all. If not, she might just as well get married, poor thing. Then we had the great reaction against feminism, and all the college girls wanted husbands and babies. During these years, marriage came to be a success symbol. If a girl failed to get her diamond ring by the second semester of her senior year, she regarded herself as a failure. There was something wrong with her. Nobody wanted her. She might as well settle for a career.

Her panic was understandable because, if she couldn't land a man on a coed college campus, how could she expect to make contact while teaching in an elementary school, or working in an office full of ineligible married men? She assumed the value of marriage—without question.

That was the style up to just a few years ago, but it's on the way out now. This year's crop of girls are playing it cool. Few of them reject the idea of marriage the way their feminist grandmothers did, but even fewer assume the superiority of home and hearth the way their mothers did. Talking with them, you get the impression that they are willing to consider marriage, but they are going to require real persuasion.

If this trend continues, we may see far fewer marriages. Both men and women will have options for other satisfying forms of life. They will have opportunities for creativity, for companionship, and for sociability. As marriages decline in number, and there are more single people, they can be expected to make their own demands upon the social order. The result may be that singleness will be regarded as being just as normal and as desirable as marriage.

And, of course, society can make good use of its single members. There are plentiful supplies of good works that can best be done by single people because of their mobility and their ability to keep themselves flexible. Francis Bacon noted, in support of the celibate priesthood, that charity can hardly water the grass when it must first fill a pool. People who have neither spouse nor children to worry about can give themselves to the work of the world with a singleminded dedication and vigor that most married people simply cannot manage. Don't forget that, as Margaret Mead has pointed out, it has traditionally been the unmarried women, such as nuns, who have taken care of the very young, the very old, and the very sick. They have been the teachers, the nurses, and the general caretakers of the society.

I am not claiming that people should give up married bliss in order to serve God or country or anything else.

That was the medieval view, which most of us have rejected. We have also rejected the medieval notion that perpetual chastity is more religious than is married life. I am merely saying that people who choose to be not married have a whole range of uses in a society. They should not have to worry about fitting in. They have their rightful place in the world, and we ought to allow them—even encourage them—to fill it.

If we ever get around to letting this happen, marriage itself will receive some real benefits from the change. When marriage becomes a matter of genuine choice—when people no longer feel that they really ought to get married because they are twenty-five, gainfully employed, and probably should settle down—then they may begin to get married for only one reason: they really want to. That will, indeed, be a great day. Just think! People getting married because they want to. It opens up whole new vistas.

First of all we may find a natural process of selectivity operating. We may find that many of our problem marriages are not getting started. The old saw that the chief cause of divorce is marriage is not too far wrong in some cases. There are many couples who should have steered clear of marriage in the first place.

Then, instead of overselling marriage as we now do, we could begin to be really honest and objective about it. We could level with single people as to what they might expect. We could begin to reduce some of our fantastic and unreal expectations so that couples could stop looking to marriage as the cure for all their ills and the salvation of their future.

We might even start to require of couples that they show some sign of genuine readiness for marriage. That brings up another old saw. It has been suggested that one way to deal with divorce is to make the grounds for marriage stiffer. Not altogether a bad idea.

Have no fear that marriage will disappear. You may be sure that even with the pressure off, most young people will probably decide to get married just the same. If we can ever reach the point where they can do it as an act of real freedom, then we will have made marriage more meaningful, both for those who decide for it and those who decide against it. After all, anybody who takes a wife to keep himself from burning, deserves all the trouble he gets.

4

Where Is the Action, Anyway?

A FEW years ago a young clergyman named Archie Hargreaves wrote a provocative article called "Go Where the Action Is." He used the language of the floating crap game to advise the contemporary church to go out into the world to find its ministry. A crap game moves from place to place, and the crap shooter has to know where the action is if he wants to stay in the game. For Hargreaves, the action today is in the ghettos, among the poor, in places where law has broken down, and in the chasms between rich and poor, black and white, city and suburbs.

The phrase has caught on widely as a symbol of dynamism, vitality, and even fun. Government and church agencies have used it to attract recruits for any number of projects. Travel agencies have used it as a slogan to tempt people to fly off to France or Italy or even Bermuda. Not too long ago, I saw on our campus a poster that read: "Go Where the Action Is—Young Republicans Fall Fling."

No doubt Mr. Hargreaves' colorful phrase has touched a responsive chord. Within the churches it has called into play powerful forces that have long been lurking in the background. For the churches in America have for some time been feeling pretty much out of it. They see themselves lumbering along on the periphery of society while the big, important things go on elsewhere. In their view "the action" seems to be wherever there are crowds of people, where decisions are being made, where power is exercised.

Though few would ever admit it, most clergymen today really pine for the restoration of the time when the pastor was at the center of things: the most highly educated man in the village, the general counselor, a leading citizen, the equal of the rich and powerful, one whose company was sought after and whose advice was taken seriously. Even the most secularized modernist in the clerical ranks likes to think of himself in this sort of role, no matter how vocally he may despise the phoniness of Christendom.

It's no wonder, then, that the minister feels frustrated in what he has come to regard as a peripheral profession, serving a peripheral institution. The church doesn't cut any ice in contemporary society, everyone seems to agree, so why waste time with it? In such a state of mind the clarion call to "go where the action is" comes with the dramatic impact of a firebell. Then what happens? Clergy left and right bug out of their parishes and head off to the big cities. Many of them take jobs with that great action agency, the Federal Government. The scuttlebutt around Washington is that OEO and the Peace Corps have more clergy on their payrolls than any of the churches have. Some head for the new frontier of the university. Others drift into social work, teaching, or administration—anyplace where the action seems to be, because wherever it is, it's certainly not in the churches. And since the churches are so hard to budge, why not just abandon ship and find the action on your own?

Anyone who has ever attended a clergy conference can testify to the prevalence of this attitude. "Here we are, off by ourselves, taking care of our own trivial knitting while the real world is going on over there somewhere. If only we could be at the center of things. If only we could participate in the decision-making process. If only we could speak to the power structures of society. But nobody listens to us. Nobody cares what we think. The church has had it. We have had it." It's beautiful, it's poignant, but is it true?

Of course, it's true. But the curious thing is that almost any group you might visit could be heard saying the same sort of things, if you caught them in the same introspective mood. Artists, musicians, and poets have had this feeling for a long, long time. Society, by the way it treats them, lets them know that they are merely expensive and dispensable luxuries, not to be taken at all seriously. Until very recently, the artists have responded in kind, accepting their assigned place outside the society and either using their work as a force for criticizing that society or sticking to their business and paying no attention to the society at all.

You might think that scientists would be exempt from this feeling. After all they occupy a prestigious position in America. Yet as you read their professional literature, you begin to realize that they, too, feel left out of things. Nobody takes their advice. Or even worse, people seek scientific advice on technical matters and then use the information in ways that the scientists would not condone. Scientists are especially suspicious of politicians, but their attitude toward the businessman is much the same. In the scientist's eyes both politicians and businessmen use them without ever taking them into the charmed circle of power. So here is a peculiar paradox: in the most scientifically oriented society in the world, the scientist himself feels left out, off at the edge of things.

Businessmen feel the same way, when they have the leisure to think about it. The government nags at them. The press doesn't treat them fairly. Certainly they never get fair treatment in literature, in the movies, or on the stage. They are everyman's scapegoat. Even their most intelligent sons decline to enter into their world because it is too sordid for their elevated tastes. If ever a group had the warrant to view itself as being at the very center of the world, it is the American business community. Yet businessmen, too, feel neglected, misunderstood, unappreciated, and left out.

So do advertising men. So do labor leaders. So do insurance men, industrial executives, lawyers, teachers, and politicians—even successful ones. Liberals and conservatives feel with special acuteness the waning power of their own tribe. Conservatives deplore the way that the "liberal establishment" has taken over the government, both political parties, the schools, the universities, the press, and everything else. Liberals at the same time see themselves as a tiny but loyal minority, fiercely hanging on by their fingernails amid the virulent attacks of the rampaging right.

Everybody is out on the edge of things. The center is always somewhere else. The power structure is in control, and we don't share the power.

Certainly this notion of "power structure" contributes to our misunderstanding of the nature of our society. The term was originally a piece of sociological shorthand to stand for the vast and complicated network of interactions that produces social decisions. It couldn't be pinned down to people, except in a very general way. The computer may change that someday, but in the meantime the whole web of relationships could be called "power structure" and the details left undefined.

But power structure is a catchy phrase and a convenient symbol. Among radicals and others who feel especially "outside," the term has taken on sinister connotations. Civil rights leaders took over the phrase, sometimes adding "white," which did nothing to clarify but managed to exempt Negroes from the sinister associations. Soon the phrase came to signify a small, tightly knit group of shadowy figures huddled over a conference table, probably in the board room of some big corporation. This little group has the power. They make the decisions. They can have things any way they want them. If things go wrong, it's their fault. So now we have both an explanation and a (partly) visible enemy.

We can best understand the way our society works if we just forget about power structure for a while. Suppose we look for the center of the society. Where will we find it? At the White House? Maybe. Maybe not. No President has ever been convinced that it was there. Congress? Certainly not. Who feels more isolated from power than a congressman? How about Wall Street—the New York Stock Exchange? Not according to the people who run it. Where, then?

The truth, I suspect, is that there isn't any center.

Part of our trouble is that we always see our society in terms of outmoded models. We are patricularly addicted to eighteenth-century models—such as an old map of Philadelphia. Now there's a city that makes sense. It is neatly bounded by two rivers. It has four sub-centers, arranged symmetrically, each marked by a small park. It has clearly defined north-south streets and east-west streets. And there, where the two principal streets come together *is* the center, visibly symbolized by that incredible pop version of the Louvre, City Hall. In this kind of city you can find your way around. You can tell where you are. You can tell whether you are at the periphery or at the center because they look different.

That's the picture most of us carry around of our society. The ambitious man—the traditional American type—starts out in life somewhere on the periphery. He tries to work his way, through one street or other, toward the center. But what happens? He doesn't find any landmarks. When he looks for City Hall, it isn't there. Or rather, first it seems to be over here, and then it's over there somewhere. All he knows is that wherever the center is, this isn't it. So he becomes confused and frustrated and assumes that he has lost his way.

But our society is nothing like eighteenth-century Philadelphia. It is much more complicated, more chaotic.

To stick to our city-map analogy, our society is more like Los Angeles. It's a collection of enclaves, held together by bands of mass communications that serve the same purpose as Los Angeles' highways. You can move from sector to sector in Los Angeles, if you have the means, but you can't really reach the center because there isn't any center. That's the story of our social life.

Now this doesn't mean that our society is any worse —or any better—than any other society at any other time. It just means that our society is different. It exists in bits and pieces, so it's harder to comprehend. You have to live differently in this sort of society. We have abandoned most of the ups and downs of the hierarchical society in favor of a vast collection of little whirlpools —or merry-go-rounds, some people might say.

If you look around, you can find plenty of evidence to bear out this analysis. You can discover all sorts of little collections of people who have their own common purposes, their own interaction, their own power distribution, their victories, and their defeats. On one level, every profession, every institution, every neighborhood is organized this way. On another level you can find the same process at work in any diner or bowling alley or corner bar. There is always a set of regulars— an in-group, the sociologist would say. They know each other, more or less, and they carry on a running conversation in their own private jargon. It will be spotted with key words or phrases, allusions and private jokes, that mean a great deal to them and very little to anyone else.

If it is a group that does anything—a voluntary organization, a political group, a labor union—it will also have its inner circle of people who influence the decisions.

That will be the power structure, if you will. In most voluntary organizations the power structure is hardly an impenetrable clique. It is more likely to be an over-worked and underappreciated collection of zealots who like nothing better than to discover a new recruit to the cause.

What does the Spirit have to say to the churches in this kind of society? I can't speak authoritatively for the Spirit, but I suspect that He might point to the real, though unconscious, element of envy in the attitude of churchmen who want to see the church right there at the center of everything. He might suggest that the churches stop trying to be City Hall—they tried that once and it didn't work out too well. He might be telling the churches to have a look around from their location out there on the periphery and take note of the fact that this is where everybody else is, too.

If this is what our society is really like, if it really is a collection of little centers of vitality, then it becomes pretty obvious what the phrase "go where the action is" must mean. It means poking around everywhere. Or, to put it another way, in a fragmented society the job of a church is to minister to the fragments. It has to forego the grandiose ambition to be the cement that welds the fragments together into a single coherent structure. That is what the medieval church tried to do. It almost worked then, but it certainly can't work now. Too much has happened since 1400.

It's a hard lesson to learn—for the church or for any-body else. As the saying goes, the hardest instrument in the world to learn to play is second fiddle. Churchmen, who possess the true word about life and death and human destiny, inevitably see their role as that of the conductor of the orchestra. But in our time the conductor's job has been abolished, and churchmen have to be content to play out their peripheral role with all the other peripheral figures: the teachers and engineers, the politicians and lawyers, and, yes, even the businessmen.

And it may turn out that the fragmented society is not such a bad thing after all. Most unified societies have had to pay a great price for their unity. Maybe now, for the first time, we can begin to accept the truth that man's purposes are inevitably at variance with each other and that the real function of the social order is to provide the best environment for men so that they can choose their own purposes, even the wrong ones, without feeling that they have to do each other in. It's a modest social theory, but not such a bad one.

Archie Hargreaves was certainly right to tell the churches to "go where the action is." And he was right to see the action where he did see it—in slums and ghettos, among the poor and exploited, and in the social cleavages between mutually alienated groups. Those are areas where the churches have not been sufficiently engaged.

But it would be a mistake to see "the action" confined to those areas. And at the same time it would be a mistake to equate "action" with power or with sheer activity. For churches bear responsibility for all the bits and pieces of the society—even the ones that don't look especially lively or attractive.

I see a lot of sentimentality about "the real world out there" among my brother clergy. Many a clergyman wants to "get out and minister to the power structures" without ever learning how to minister to the power structure that constitutes his own board, vestry, or women's organization. Many others are convinced that somewhere else there is a *center* where all the subliminal forces in the society come into focus. But the plain fact is that there isn't any center. Wherever you go, you're still going to be out at the edge of things.

But the opposite is also true. If there is no one center, there are centers all over. Where the action is, is everywhere. If you are really looking for action, you can certainly find it in the inner city, as Mr. Hargreaves so convincingly demonstrates. But you can also find it in the small town and in the country and even—if you look—in the much-abused suburb.

So by all means, go where the action is. There is no telling where you may end up—in East Harlem or at the Young Republicans Fall Fling, or right where you are. And maybe then you'll discover that the real issue is not where the action is, but what you're going to do once you've found it.

5

From the Underground
to the Establishment

Aᖴᴛᴇʀ the word had gotten around my neighborhood that, contrary to anyone's reasonable expectation, I was about to leave my job and go into seminary to study for the ministry, I was accosted one day by a quaint elderly gentleman who, predictably, clucked his approval of this new move. Then he added: "I'm so glad to hear that you're going into the ministry. You'll get to meet such lovely people."

I've thought about that prediction during the years that followed. On the whole, I'd have to say the old boy was right. I have met some lovely people. I've met quite a few of all sorts, from the terribly intellectual graduate student who interpreted my sermon on the Resurrection to mean that I believed in reincarnation to the smooth-talking Latin who cheated me out of one hundred dollars of my discretionary fund (or, as one of my friends put it, my indiscretionary fund).

Whether or not my experience has been typical, I would not venture to judge. But since I am a clergyman, and since I have been based on a college campus for some years, I suspect that my contacts may tend to run to extremes. I don't mean just different kinds of individuals. I am more conscious of the radical differences among groups—the ways they think, the beliefs and attitudes they hold, the things they regard as important, and the way they look at each other. As you move from one such group to a very different kind of group, you sometimes get a weird feeling that you have lost contact with reality. For what you were ready to consider as terribly significant in that group becomes quite unreal in this one. Or what is regarded as urgent and serious business in this group has been the butt of ridicule in that one.

It is hard to catalogue the worlds, but some of them stand out with special clarity. There is the world of what *Time* magazine has called "The Command Generation"—the business and professional people who run things. They dominate church structures as they dominate the rest of our society. There is a special world of culture and the arts. It has its own command generation with a different set of concerns and priorities.

There is a special little world of politics, filled with meetings, mailings, and maneuvers. The world of youth has its own particular set of attitudes and values. There is a world of academe with its special subgroups, consisting of students or faculty or administrators. And within academe, but spilling over into the world of urban bohemia, is a special underground of disaffected intellectuals and political radicals.

Everyone admits that society is split up into smaller groups. Call it fragmented, if you want to be *au courant*. But what is hard for the outsider to understand is just how unreal the rest of the world seems when you look at it from the perspective of one specific group. We are all aware of the tendency to deal in stereotypes, but it comes as a shock when you realize just how stereotyped the stereotypes are. When you hear one of these "discussions by pigeonhole" that concerns people whom you know in the flesh, you are likely to get the feeling that you have been trapped in some great distortion mirror that speaks the truth, but in no recognizable fashion.

I've been working around college students for a long time, and through the years I've been hearing about parents. The parents of college students are perhaps the most unattractive lot of human beings on God's green earth—to hear their children tell about them. Students' attitudes toward their parents range all the way from open hostility to good-humored indulgence. From their conversation you get a composite picture of The Parent. He likes Doris Day movies because they have happy endings. He makes bum jokes about modern art. He's devoted to Mantovani and phony early American furniture. His idea of a real intellectual feast is to spend an evening with the *Reader's Digest*. He sees himself as a middle-of-the-roader in politics but is very suspicious of anything "radical." His political attitude is summed up in the phrase, "Nothing too fast." He goes to church regularly, but his only real spiritual commitment is to the supreme value of making a buck. He's obviously a hopeless square, but at the same time he's a tyrant who forces his shallow values on his more deeply thoughtful children.

I used to buy this picture uncritically because it was drawn by intelligent youngsters who seemed to be pretty perceptive about most other things. But I would often get to wondering how such cruddy parents could ever turn out such fundamentally decent and sensitive kids. And when I got to meet parents, they would often turn out to look like fairly decent and sensitive people.

I never really figured this one out until my own friends began to reach the age at which you begin to send your children to college. I was struck by the fact that the children of my most alert and sophisticated friends always regarded them as the same hopeless squares I had been hearing about for years. I can think of several couples I know who are widely read, who keep up with politics, the arts, music, and drama, whose opinions are advanced on most fronts, who in fact were the student radicals of a generation ago. But to hear their children talk, you would think they were all Babbitts who never cared about anything more important than the next Rotary meeting.

Yes, college students do have their prejudices against the adult world, and they are not confined to parents. The adults in the university itself come in for some rough treatment. Faculty are, by and large, exempt from the universal condemnation. I can't imagine why. Any student worth his salt knows that students and teachers are natural enemies. But the students' hostilities have been deflected by the intervention of a third force (probably created for that very purpose): The Administration.

There is absolutely no point in telling a student that

The Administration is only a group of people hired to count the money and make the wheels go 'round. No, The Administration is not people. It is a gray, faceless entity, fanatically devoted to blocking and frustrating the student at every turn. It won't let him have cars or beer or girls in his dorm room. It makes him wait in line to register. It feeds him bad food. It raises his tuition. It makes all sorts of silly rules about grades and cuts and required courses that no right-thinking student would ever take of his own free will. It interferes with his social life, his political activity, even his education.

Such omnipotent malevolence must surely stem from an overwhelmingly intelligent maliciousness (or malicious intelligence). The crimes of The Administration are so great that they raise real questions as to its humanity. No wonder the average student believes that his university is really run by a mad computer named Charlie.

How strange it is when you meet one of these sinister powers, and he turns out to be disappointingly human —often even normal. Administrators tend to be generally honest, kind to their wives and children, and fairly well-disposed toward people. Surprisingly many of them are men of liberal convictions. Some of them are men of real stature.

Of course, university administrators have some occupational diseases. They tend to be defensive and rather too quick to respond to criticism. Of course, they get so much that it makes them edgy. Then, too, most administrators are likely to be very sensitive about their image. But that is not too hard to understand. They have a lot of people to keep happy: trustees, parents, alumni, prospective donors, church or state officials, and even the general public. They hardly have time left to wonder what the students think.

It would have to be conceded that administrators have an incurable tendency to look at students with a rather jaundiced eye. Since students work on the time-tested principle that the squeaky wheel gets the grease, administrators come to regard all students as squeaky wheels. Out of their vast fund of experience, they usually relate to the student on the basis of, "I wonder what he's trying to get away with." Unfortunately, their fears are often only too well founded.

So it becomes clear that the young folks have certain irrational prejudices against the older generation. But that is to be expected because, after all, they are young and you can't tell them anything. They are convinced that anyone more than twenty-five years old is dead. They are full of youthful zeal and idealism. They are self-confident to the point of arrogance, as any forty-year-old knows. But you can always take heart in the saying attributed to Mark Twain: "When I was seventeen, I was sure my father didn't know anything. But when I got to be twenty-one, I was surprised to discover how much the old man had learned in four years."

Thank God we adults have gotten over such a one-sided view of the world. We understand youth because we have been through it. We have outgrown stereo-typed thinking. We judge people on their own merits. We are wise in the ways of the world.

Funny, but you would never know it from listening to the middle-aged established classes talk about youth. I'm sure you've heard the party line. It goes something like this: "Oh sure, most of them are nice clean kids, but those beatnik types! You know, with the beards and long, dirty hair. They dress sloppily and go barefoot. At least they could wash once in a while. They don't have any discipline. They never heard of responsibility or ambition or even patriotism. They play around with fads like LSD and Zen Buddhism. They smoke pot or take even worse things. They have all sorts of kooky political ideas. They want to do away with everything, but they don't have any substitutes to offer. And worst of all, they are all preoccupied with SEX!"

I've lost count of the times I've heard that monologue, with minor variations. If you think the prejudices of youth are hard to crack, just try working on the OK world's prejudices against youth. Of course, the young don't help their cause very much. They often seem determined to act out their opposition to society in the most flamboyant ways they can dream up. They manage to add plausibility to the stereotypes, even while they are protesting against them.

I would be the first to admit that I have a hard time doing business with these people. Of course, I am over twenty-five, and they never let you forget that. Wearing a clerical collar is certainly no help. It automatically sets you apart as a visible representative of the world of home and mother and all the rest. Yet, when we do get our respective guards down, the result is sometimes refreshing, and I've managed to learn some things from the exposure.

For one thing I'm not convinced that our new generation of middle-class radicals is about to reject the middle class. To hear their rhetoric it seems clear that the middle class is The Enemy. No doubt the phrase "middle class" carries the same sort of symbolic power that the phrase "power structure" carries for the out-of-power Negro.

What the student radical rejects is not the middle class *per se*, but rather a constellation of attitudes that many middle-class people hold, often without thinking much about the matter. He rejects such things as petty moralism; the provincial complacency that makes it so hard for affluent people to recognize that anything could be wrong with the world; the rigidity that makes it harder for older established people to change their minds or their attitudes. Most important, he resents the way in which so many middle-class people have insulated themselves in their pleasant, gadget-filled world and have ignored the whole other world of poverty, problems, and pathos.

After he has been in the university for a while, the more sensitive student may begin to question the assumption that education is the final cure for the world's ills. He knows it hasn't cured his own ills, so he begins to suspect that he's been had. At the same time he begins to wonder about the validity of what his parents have taught him, especially their view that affluence is the goal of life.

But the characteristic of middle-class life that infuriates the radical student is that it seems so settled. It is finished with traveling or seeking. It has no spirit of adventure, no capacity for risk. Then he begins to be wary of getting trapped himself. This is why he is so likely to give himself over to protest, demonstration, and activism. He wants to get hold of real issues and live real life among real people.

I don't see that this points to any rejection of the really important values of the middle-class world. Young radicals take many middle-class values for granted without noticing where they originated. Their sympathy for the underdog, for example, is in the American tradition. Their hopefulness, which strikes the hardened oldster as incredibly naïve, is something that has been in the culture for a long time. They are generally honest, forthright, and far more benevolent than their sometimes extravagant language would seem to suggest.

Even the wild political ideas of the "new left" are by no means as antitraditional as they sound. The noisiest of them are only asking to have applied to the society those democratic processes about which we've been talking for more than a century. What is new about their view is that they are more consistent in their democratic ideology than any group in the nation has ever been before. They might be "leftist" as they claim, but they are a far cry from the dogmatic Marxist left of thirty years ago.

As a group they may be as naïve as their critics have painted them, but I am not so sure. It is true that they have never held power, and, consequently, their acquaintance with responsibility is on a pretty primitive level. But I have been quite impressed with their knowledgeability. They have a staggering amount of information at their fingertips, and they know how to make use of it. They read the books they talk about. They keep up with the newspapers and journals. If you want to argue with any of these lads, you had better do your homework and get your facts straight or they will make you feel pretty silly.

It is an interesting experience to shuttle back and forth from the underground to the establishment. I frequently find myself in one group operating from the presuppositions of the other. As a result I'm left feeling like a fish out of water much of the time. Whenever I hear those diatribes about beatniks or the stodgy middle class, I find myself starting to say, "Yes, but . . . ," but somehow it doesn't get heard.

I cannot guess how we should try to paper over these cracks in the great society. It's easy enough to utter the magic word, "communication," but that just states the problem. It would be nice to think you could bring them all together, the hip and the square, the radical underground and the conservative establishment, so that they could learn at first hand from each other. I've tried that on occasion and it doesn't work. The conversation quickly becomes polarized, communication breaks down, and both groups go away with their worst suspicions confirmed.

If you agree that this fragmentation presents a problem, you might try a little experiment in your own corner of the vineyard. Find yourself a group that you really don't dig: the hippies, the discotheque set, the New Left, the Chamber of Commerce, the AMA, or the American Legion. Look for ways to penetrate the outfit. Hang around them and get in on the conversation. Don't worry about making points. Just keep your ears open until you can see them in the way that they see themselves. If you hang on long enough, you'll eventually get tuned in to their wavelength. If you do, I guarantee you will find yourself looking at some new things in a new way. If you're an antibourgeois student, you may find that there is some life in the old folks yet. If you're irrevocably middle class and irretriveably middle aged, it may make you feel young again. In any case if you're lucky, you may get to meet some lovely people.

6

Right You Are
(If You Say So):

Mass Communications and
the Self-fulfilling Prophecy

IGHT You Are (If You Think So), Luigi Pirandello's well-known play, embodies that playwright's own peculiar view of reality. The play
presents conflicting accounts of the same event. According to the playwright, each version is "true" because
someone believes it to be true, for reality is whatever the
mind chooses to regard as real. The age of instant mass
communications has improved upon Pirandello by developing a device that can produce truth on demand: the
self-fulfilling prophecy.

Of course, we've been used to having prophets around
for a long, long time. They go back at least to Samuel,
who lived somewhere around 1000 B.C. Diviners and
soothsayers go back much further than that. People have

always wanted to know in advance what was going to happen, and down through history they have heaped honors and prestige upon the man who could establish a claim to reading the future.

Divination, however, has always been a risky enterprise. When you're good, things are fine. People pay you well, and they generally take your advice. But when you make a mistake, it's likely to be a real whopper. Then you go down in history, but not the way most people want to go. We can recall some of the more obvious bloopers: the nineteenth-century Commissioner of the U.S. Patent Office who wanted to close up shop because everything imaginable had already been invented; Herbert Hoover, after the stock-market crash, confidently predicting that "prosperity is just around the corner"; the *Literary Digest* announcing in 1936 that Alf M. Landon was going to defeat Roosevelt; H. V. Kaltenborn solemnly proclaiming the election of Thomas E. Dewey in 1948. When you see how silly an inaccurate prediction appears in retrospect, you wonder if it wouldn't be better to keep your big mouth shut.

But the hazards of prediction are now being eliminated by the development of communications technology, so that the latter-day prophet is in a stronger position. Today, any prediction is likely to be disseminated widely through television, radio, newspapers, and magazines. A popular prophet will get the kind of hearing that puts his prediction before vast numbers of people who have no way of checking up on the accuracy of the prediction or on the credentials of the predictor. As word gets around that a certain thing is going to happen, enough people may act on that assumption to make the thing actually happen. You might put it this way: the original prophets were valued because they could read the mysterious "handwriting on the wall." Today's prophets are often in a position to put the handwriting there in the first place.

During the Eisenhower Administration, Secretary of the Treasury George Humphrey was severely criticized for his public statements about government fiscal policies. At one point he complained that such wasteful spending could only lead to a depression that would "curl your hair." In the controversy that followed, the question of whether Humphrey was right or wrong was lost in the clamor over the advisability of the statement. The consensus was that he shouldn't have said it. Why not? Because a statement like that, coming from someone in authority, could destroy business confidence. A wave of selling on the stock market might follow, and if it did we might in fact have a hair-curling depression that we would not have otherwise had. In other words, people feared the prophecy because they thought that it might fulfill itself.

Business confidence is the most sensitive respondent to the self-fulfilling prophecy. That, of course, is why the IN party always exudes self-confidence no matter what the economic climate, while the OUTS, who criticize current economic policies, are always pictured as prophets of gloom who are out to destroy the fragile confidence of the business community.

That, too, is why Herbert Hoover continued to predict the imminent coming of prosperity until the very end of his term of office. He was no more naïve than anyone else, but he knew that whatever else it might take to get the country out of depression, it would certainly take confidence and plenty of it. If people could be led to believe that prosperity was really just around that corner, then by golly it might really be there. When you think about it, Franklin Roosevelt's memorable phrase in his inaugural address, "We have nothing to fear but fear itself," was in much the same vein—and directed toward the same end—as Hoover's pronouncements. The difference was that the nation listened to Roosevelt and believed him. The prophecy was on the way to self-fulfillment.

Politics, like economics, abounds in self-fulfilling prophecies. The band-wagon effect in elections is based on the view that if enough people believe that a candidate is going to win, he will. It didn't turn out that way in 1948, to be sure, but then nothing is foolproof. But a new and disturbing variation of the band-wagon effect has recently been produced by the combination of the voting machine and the television set.

Some of the densely populated states of the northeast vote entirely by machine. Connecticut, for example, has its returns in, fairly completely, even before the polls have closed in the West Coast states. Television is able to carry the returns to the West so that many people have a good indication of how things are going in the election even before they have voted. If your candidate appears beaten before you have even voted, will you bother to vote at all? No one knows for sure. But there is some indication that the eastern vote acts upon the western voter as something very like a self-fulfilling prophecy.

Likewise, many political scientists have expressed the thought that public-opinion polls shape opinion even as they record it. If seventy-two percent of the people are recorded as being in favor of a proposal or policy, the subtle implication is that this is "what everybody thinks" or, even more subtly, "what all right-thinking people think." If your own view is contrary, you may begin to feel that there is no use in talking about the issue because everyone is probably on the other side. Then, as your minority voice dies out, your view becomes discredited and set aside without ever having been heard. The public-opinion poll has acted the role of prophet and has enabled its prophecy to fulfill itself.

In every area of life there is a tendency for actuality to follow our impressions of it. If enough people begin to say that old Jones's business is on the skids, sure enough it will skid, sooner or later. Crime apparently follows crime news just as surely as crime news follows crime. How we think about things depends largely upon the image we have of them, which is why so many people, institutions, and nations are concerned as much about their image as about their actual condition.

In the world of higher education, it is no secret that institutions can coast for years, even generations, on their reputations. Here it is especially easy to do, since the hard realities about quality in a university are very hard to come by. The standards are vague and contradictory. How good is Harvard, really? Nobody knows, really. But then, it doesn't make much difference. So long as enough people think that Harvard is the Greatest University in the World, it will be. The best students will fight to enroll there. The best scholars will jump at the chance to work there. So Harvard can't lose. If your students measure up well, and if you have enough well-known and respected scholars on your faculty, you are good by definition.

Ah, but suppose the impossible were to happen. Suppose word began to get around to the effect that dear old

Harvard has had it. Then suppose that without any change in the realities, people began to believe it. Then what would happen? Top-notch students would begin to have second thoughts before they would accept admission to Harvard. Bright young scholars might decline to accept appointments there. Large donors might begin to put their money elsewhere. Perhaps even the Federal Government would stop making research grants to Harvard. In a very short time, Harvard would find itself in a real decline.

If this could happen to Harvard, what about every other institution? The same thing could happen to any one of them, of course, which is what makes them all a little nervous. Universities are, by and large, the most PR-conscious institutions in the land because so much depends upon their public image. Since there is no way in the world to project what is best in a university, all it can do is grind out the pollyanna propaganda and hope for the best. If you read the literature, then, you discover that every university in the nation is moving boldly forward, building for the future on the basis of a proud and noble tradition. If there is no tradition on which to build, then the future just looks that much rosier. Not every prophecy can be self-fulfilling, but if any university president were to share with the public his anxieties about the future, he would soon find he had plenty to be anxious about.

On another level the world of higher education provides an illustration of the self-fulfilling prophecy in the great admissions crush. When the baby boom of the 1940's began to hit college age, word soon got around that it was becoming harder and harder to get accepted by the college of your choice. Soon there were all sorts of panic stories suggesting that there were too few places for too many students. Consequently many qualified aspirants were going to be left behind.

What happened? Naturally the people who believed the stories took measures to defend themselves. They would apply to three, four, or a dozen different colleges, just to be safe. As a result the colleges began to get huge volumes of additional applications until they were almost buried under the avalanche. But at the same time they could not afford to rely on the applications they did accept. If you wanted a thousand freshmen, you would have to accept anywhere from fifteen hundred, if you were a prestige college, to twenty-five hundred or more. You knew in advance that many of your acceptances would be going to students who would be accepted by two to five other colleges.

So, then, predictions of a great admissions crush helped to produce the crush that followed. Certainly there was truth to the reports about the scarcity of places, but what is important is that the report itself carried its own built-in verification factor. It couldn't go wrong. If there had been no admissions crush, the prediction might well have invented one.

In a more sensitive area we have had a rash of summer riots in a number of cities. The riots started back in 1964, but there have been a few more each year. Every year along about spring, we begin to hear about this or that intolerable condition which simply must be alleviated or we will be having riots in the long, hot summer. Granted the complaints are legitimate and the intolerable conditions are real, nevertheless the riots are new. And there is no doubt that news about riots and predictions about riots have something to do with the emergence of riots.

Any alert slumdweller who reads the newspapers might well conclude that he really ought to pull off a riot to keep his self-respect.

The student riots and demonstrations that have recently spread east from Berkeley, California, have partaken of some of the same contrived spontaneity. After all, what campus does not have something to complain about? There have been complaints as long as there have been students. Before Berkeley, however, hardly anyone would have thought that a massive demonstration on a sophisticated contemporary college campus would have had any chance of success. But Berkeley opened up a whole new range of possibilities for the campus political type, and he quickly took the cue. Again we find reality conforming to our view of it.

The Protestant churches today find themselves in the midst of a crisis of confidence which they may have had a share in producing. Seminaries, for example, report a general decline in the number of applications for admission during the past few years. Church attendance throughout the nation has, at the same time, begun to dip. This comes as no surprise, since a number of critics have been predicting for years that this was going to happen. The critics have been mostly Protestant theologians. Their cry has been that the church is doomed because its activities are frivolous, its message irrelevant, and its way of life uncongenial to the modern temper.

Statistics are now beginning to bear out their predictions. But could it also be that their predictions have something to do with the statistics? If you have been hearing for years, from men you respect and admire, that the church is a haven for conventional hypocrisy, that Protestantism in America is on the way out, that the ministry is a dying trade, wouldn't you think twice before devoting your life to being a clergyman? And if you've been told, over and over again, that the only reason people seek out the church is to find friends, or self-identity, or security in a chancy world, wouldn't you feel just a bit sheepish coming around to church on Sunday mornings? The rather intense and often bad-tempered criticism of Protestantism by Protestant theologians has produced its own set of self-fulfilling prophecies. When the fishmonger cries "rotten fish," people are likely to take him at his word. And if the same fishmonger predicts a rapid falling off of fish sales, is it any occasion for wonder when that is what actually happens?

The self-fulfilling prophecy is really nothing new. People of power and influence have known about it for a long time. Their way of dealing with it is simple: you just say over and over what you want to be true; then maybe it will become true. This sounds very much like what we used to call superstition, I know, but in this electronic age, it works more often than we realize.

This is why economists—especially those in official positions—are always predicting that this year's gross national product will exceed last year's and that, in spite of a twelve-point drop in the Dow-Jones average, the stock market is really basically sound and healthy. This is why Secretary of Defense McNamara had to make all those embarrassingly cheerful proclamations, a few years ago, to the effect that we were winning the war in Vietnam, and it would all be over in a year or so. You can argue about his reliability—or even his good sense—but you have to admit that if he had predicted that we were going to lose the war in a year, we probably would have.

As a result of Secretary McNamara's remarks—and

other similar optimistic handouts—the Johnson Administration has been suffering from the effects of what newsmen call a "credibility gap." Translated, it simply means that if you catch people in enough lies, you stop believing them. This is the common man's reaction to the expert's reaction to the self-fulfilling prophecy. Common man gets used to the idea that public statements are made not to provide information, but to create an effect. He quickly learns to discount the information in the statement and to ask, instead, "I wonder what reaction that statement is supposed to produce." You might say that common man begins to regard all public statements as commercials of one sort or another.

So now look at the mess we're in. Because a statement has the power of persuasion, it can produce the effect it predicts. The man who knows this will make statements calculated to produce the effect he wants. But his hearers know that this is what he is up to, so they tend to discount his statement. If enough people discount what he has to say, his statement won't have the desired effect and so endeth the self-fulfilling prophecy.

This process is well under way already. I recently heard a lecture dealing with citizenship in a democracy in which the speaker was calling for a well-informed citizenry. He went on to make the usual comment: "Isn't it too bad that so many of our people don't read the papers. They just read the comics and the sports pages."

One student, obviously the new breed, remarked wryly that the sports page and the comics are the only parts of the newspaper you can trust.

The credibility gap is with us to stay, I fear. On the other hand, I don't really fear it at all. The growing skepticism of common man is encouraging because it shows that people can still adapt themselves to new circumstances. They know when they've been had, and they find ways to fight back.

That's all to the good because, in this never-never land of statement-for-effect, plain old-fashioned truth takes an awful beating. Of course, you can maintain that in a pragmatic sense statements are true if they produce the desired effect. That is, although they may be objectively false, they may be operationally true. That's a neat bit of rationalization, but it's hardly what William James meant by his pragmatic test for truth. I doubt that it's an adequate test for most of us either. To most of our simple minds, it sounds very much like manipulative double-talk. And if we can keep that kind of nonsense from gaining ground, we will all be much better off.

7

The Power of
Negative Thinking

THE Norman Vincent Peale fad peaked and sub-
sided some time ago, but even now Dr. Peale
rates as one of the most popular and influential
clergymen of our era. His message has been a simple
proclamation: You can, if you will only believe you can.
Positive thinking, he maintained, produces its own power
which can banish anxiety and lead to self-confidence and
success. Dr. Peale's books are full of stories telling how
defeated and despairing men have found themselves and
have gone on to enjoy life, to achieve their goals, and—
usually—to make money.

That message of hope and comfort was welcomed
with enthusiasm in an age characterized by longing and
uncertainty. Thousands have flocked to hear Dr. Peale's

sermons. Hundreds of thousands bought his books. His most successful work, *The Power of Positive Thinking,* sold over a million copies in the middle fifties.

But through the years, Dr. Peale has had his critics, too. William Lee Miller took out after him as early as 1954. Dr. Miller was soon followed by Wayne Oates, A. Roy Eckhart, Martin Marty, and Will Herberg—all respectable theologians, historians, or social critics. One sociologist found Dr. Peale's doctrines so distasteful that he dismissed them with a contemptuous phrase and refused to discuss them at all.

The main charges against Dr. Peale were, first, that in claiming that a man could will himself into achievement, Dr. Peale failed to take into account the tragic dimension of life, the fact that reality cannot be made to respond to our mental gymnastics. Second, Dr. Peale tended to equate moral victory with social and financial success. For Dr. Peale, the gospel promise seemed to have been translated into bank accounts and power symbols.

Now I could never quite see myself breaking a lance in defense of Dr. Peale, but I would maintain that in spite of the gaucheries and the distortions involved in his position, he did have hold of something valid. I was never convinced that his formula for success could really deliver the goods, but that is not the issue. The kernel of truth in all this is that, although positive thinking may not be able to set you up, negative thinking can surely do you in. The power of positive thinking is still in doubt, but the power of negative thinking is beyond dispute.

We have noticed that a prophecy of doom is more likely to fulfill itself than a more hopeful prediction. Gloomy talk can bring on depression—economic or psychological—quicker than cheerful chatter can dispel it. Predictions of military defeat, social panic, or rioting in the streets are likely to be fulfilled on schedule, whereas pained embarrassment is more likely to be the lot of those who insist that nothing can go wrong, go wrong, go wrong.

It's the same in our daily lives, as the preachers say. Back in the happy days of radio, there was a comedian named Al Pierce, who used to do a bit featuring "the world's worst traveling salesman." He would sneak up to a door, ring the bell, and mutter, "Afraid there's nobody to home here, I hope, I hope, I hope." Needless to say, he earned his title.

I used to know a boy who would approach every new situation with that same attitude. Whatever it was, he was sure it was going to be too much for him. If he were learning to play a new game, he'd start off by announcing, "Oh, I don't think I can do that." When he would make his first mistake, he would say, "See? I told you it was too hard." Then, after a few more mistakes, he would quit in utter frustration and despair.

What hurt was that he had real ability, but he never gave himself a chance. He was so convinced of the inevitability of failure that he would never marshal his resources, never take pains, never strive valiantly in the face of defeat. He would play around with the new thing until it gave him trouble. Then he'd go out like a fighter with a glass jaw.

It was like that with everything. Life was simply too much to bear. It was all Problem. So, in any encounter he was licked before he could start. As Dr. Peale would have pointed out, he was beaten by his own attitude before the problem could ever get to him. The power of negative thinking had done its dastardly work.

A critic of Dr. Peale once quoted at length from a story in which Dr. Peale told how he had encountered a young

Negro boy who was convinced that because he was a Negro, he had no future. Dr. Peale saw that he had a strong arm, a quick mind, and a ready smile. He told the boy that great possibilities lay before him. Look at Ralph Bunche. Look at Jackie Robinson. You can do it, too. The critic thought that this attitude was naïve and irresponsible. It would foster unhealthy illusions. It would lead that boy to hopes that the future could not fulfill.

Well, we can all concede the hardships involved in being a young Negro man in America today. But how helpful would it be to encourage that boy in his discouragement? Those who work with young Negro high school dropouts tell us that their greatest problem is to convince the kids that there is some point to their struggle. They try to build up a sense of expectation in the boys so that they will want to develop. They can't do that unless the boys themselves are persuaded to believe in the future. When they become convinced that life is going to cave in on them, it does.

Of course, I wouldn't claim that positive thinking can remove all the obstacles to peace and happiness. But it might help us over some unnecessary hurdles, those that our own uncertainties put in our way. After all, every situation in life comes to us bearing both threat and promise alike. When you take an examination, you risk failure but you may pass a real landmark. Moving into a new city may require you to leave old friends behind, but it also opens up the possibility of developing new relationships. A family quarrel may breed bitterness and resentment, but it may also resolve a conflict or clear up a misunderstanding. How we move to meet such situations depends largely upon how we perceive them. You can view any situation as a promise that has a few problems thrown in, or you can see it as a problem that may have a few mitigating circumstances.

When all you can see in a situation is the possibility of risk, threat, and failure, then you are very likely to shrink from it. Then your style disappears. You falter when you need to make a bold stroke. You evade when you should charge in. You get upset when you make a mistake. Finally you get so discouraged that it becomes easier to quit than to keep on going.

I don't know why this should be so. Maybe when you confront a new situation timidly, you are really telegraphing down into your unconscious frantic signals that read: "Help! Get me out of here!" And deep down there some anonymous collection of cells replies, "That can be arranged." Then they call over to your motor centers and static up the signals so that you fall all over your feet and compound the problem.

It works easily enough on the interpersonal level. You often see parents who have started off half-scared of their children. They have read all the literature, and they know everything that can go wrong. They are sure that the kids are all going to end up as juvenile delinquents, or worse. So whenever the children do anything wrong, as children sometimes will, the parents overreact out of their own fears. Of course, then, the children overreact to their reaction and the battle is on. If the children do become delinquent, the parents' anxieties will have had something to do with it.

A colleague of mine once told me about a counseling experience he had with a man who had no self-confidence. He had finished college, but had never caught on. He had lost his job and was having trouble in finding another. My friend saw him regularly over a long period during which he slipped further and further down. The longer he was without a job the worse he felt, and the worse he felt the harder it was for him to get a job. It was six months before my friend found out the worst. The man was so convinced that nobody would hire him that he had never even tried to get a job. He was certain it would be no use to ask. Oh, he would comb the classified ads regularly every day. He would visit places and ask if they were hiring. But he never asked for a single interview. He never made a single appointment. He never even filed a single application.

I should end this story in true Dr. Peale fashion by adding that the man finally did get his confidence back, found a job and now makes forty thousand dollars a year. But it wouldn't be true. Actually the man became so upset when my friend pinned him down on the facts that he never came back.

I suspect that all the positive thinking in the world would never have made that man into a forty-thousand-dollar-a-year commodity. But it is clear that his lack of self-confidence was a most formidable foe. My point is that before we write off Dr. Peale and his followers, we have to concede them this much: a hopeful, positive stance is at least an important precondition for doing business in this world. It won't guarantee success—whatever that is. But its absence will go a long way toward guaranteeing failure.

I don't mean to sound like Pollyanna. There are, after all, situations that turn out to be all threat and no promise. But even so when you look at people who have problems, what strikes you is that the size of their problem seldom corresponds to the impact that it has on them.

I once watched a man die of cancer. His last days were full of constant pain and discomfort. Yet through it all, he kept his courage with an unfailing good humor that would have done credit to many a man in more happy circumstances. On the other hand we have all known people who go into a swivet over a simple headache. Why is it that some people can meet tragedy with grace and aplomb, while others cannot rise above even a petty annoyance? Maybe there is something to the old saying that the size of a man can be measured by what it takes to throw him off balance.

There are plenty of people around who serve very nicely as their own worst enemy. During the existentialism vogue, the college campuses were full of healthy and vigorous young men and women all curled up in cocoons contemplating their interior self or waiting for the *eschaton*. Most of the ones I knew were youngsters who had a lot going for them: health, affluence, intelligence, good education, and considerable freedom of choice— things that people throughout the world were willing to die for. But there they were, groveling helplessly in *angst* and wondering whether to commit suicide.

The existentialists have had their day, but the suburban-housewife syndrome is still with us. You know, "Here I am in my new split-level with a loving husband and three darling children and enough money to get by on, but I find I have nothing to live for." And she sits around all day being anxious. Or she hits the bottle—or the kids.

Then there's the rejected-mother syndrome. This is a disease that sometimes hits the middle-class mother when her children have grown, and she's left with nothing to do. She has packed them all off to college or, worse yet, has gotten them all safely married and out of the nest. Then she sits down in her quiet, empty house and wrings her hands. Nothing to do. Nobody needs me. Nothing to live for. On through the dreary years she goes, feeling genuinely sorry for herself, for her lot is surely grievous. In such cases I recommend a good, stiff dose of Dr. Norman Vincent Peale. Don't take the whole bottle. It may produce hallucinations. But a little nip of positive thinking won't do any harm. After all, it *is* better to be healthy than to be starving, better to be safe than to live in terror, better to be surrounded by love, however demanding, than to live in the midst of hatred and malice.

I'm not ready to go the whole way with Dr. Peale, by any means. And I really am sorry if I've begun to sound like Elbert Hubbard or the latest *Reader's Digest*. I am certainly not ready to opt for Pollyanna as my guide through this vale of tears.

But I do think that the case against negative thinking is airtight. The danger of self-paralysis is, at this moment in history, far more serious than the danger of self-delusion. In fact, I suspect that even Dr. Peale's own following is composed largely of negative thinkers who are willing to try anything to help them throw off the habit.

Maybe you can accuse Dr. Peale of failing to deliver. I don't know how much real effect he has had. But I'm not ready to throw too many rocks at him because, though he may have overstated his case, though he may have accepted too uncritically the notions of success currently held in America, though he may have underestimated the difficulty in bringing about real changes in men's attitudes, nevertheless, he does indeed have something there. Positive thinking may not change the world but, taken in small doses, it may help us to put our overwhelming burdens into perspective. If we can do that, maybe we will begin to see that most of our troubles don't amount to that much after all.

8

The Morality Game

THE most frequent diagnosis of our era is that we live in a time of declining morals, a time when conventional notions of right and wrong are breaking down. People, it is commonly said, don't behave the way they used to. Business is full of greed; government is full of corruption; the schools are full of cheating; people drink too much; they get too many divorces; and the young folks are all smoking pot.

Like most other nonanalytic people, I find that hard to believe. I'm not sure that we are any worse off than, say, the Victorian age, which seems so neat and strait-laced now that it's over. We would certainly compare favorably with Renaissance Italy or Restoration England. Maybe we won't go down in history as the Puritan Generation, but I doubt that we are much worse than most.

We have had a few noteworthy developments in our views of morality in recent years. Free-living schools of morality have appeared, expressing the conviction that if you do as you please, you'll find true freedom and happiness—and you'll enjoy better digestion at the same time. In spite of the way this notion gets distorted by its less imaginative proponents, it may have something to it.

On another front we've witnessed the advent of something called the "New Morality." I don't know exactly what it is. Professor Joseph Fletcher has recently published a book called *Situation Ethics*, which carries the subtitle: "The New Morality"; but it doesn't shed much light on the subject. All he tells us is that Christians should always act out of love even though they have to break the rules. If he means only that the Christian ethic is a love ethic, I would agree with him, but I would have to complain that there is nothing much new in that morality. St. Augustine said pretty much the same thing more than fifteen hundred years ago.

Certainly Dr. Fletcher's complaint about the "rules" is valid. Not that there is anything wrong with rules *per se*. We operate according to rules most of the time, and they don't hurt us much. "Pay your bills." "Stay on the right-hand side of the road." "Don't hit a man when he's down." "Don't put water in the beer." Rules have their uses. The trouble starts when we confuse the rules with morality.

It's time we took a fresh look at this business of rules and morality. If we want a way to get into the problem, we might well take a hint from Dr. Eric Berne, whose delightful book *Games People Play* has inhabited the best-seller lists for more than a year.

No wonder the book has been so popular. Aside from being the first psychiatrist who ever betrayed a sense of humor about his business, Dr. Berne has something important to say. In his group-therapy sessions he learned to make use of operations analysis and game theory. As a result he was able to identify a whole collection of games people play, consciously or unconsciously, to make their way in the world, to defend themselves against the slings and arrows of outrageous fortune.

In this theory a game consists of a series of operations with a specific goal. It requires a number of players, each of whom has a role to play. In order for the game to work, each player has to observe a set of unspoken rules. Most important, according to Dr. Berne, a game includes an ulterior motive. That is, the person who starts the game wants something out of it, some special satisfaction or the fulfillment of some specific need.

I would suggest that many of the rules that people call morality are best understood in terms of the games people play. In a simple-minded sort of way this is nothing new. Theodore Roosevelt used to talk about morality as "playing the game." Sportsmanship, in this view, was more than mere sportsmanship. It was a way of being moral. At that time, though, there wasn't much doubt as to what the game was. It was the Great Game of Life, and if you played it right you reached the goal of Success, and everybody knew what that was.

Today, life is a little more complicated. We have been overwhelmed by a proliferation of games. We have thousands to choose from, like brands of toothpaste in the supermarket. The great problem of the age is not that morality is declining. The problem is that we are suffering from a boom in morality games.

Much of the static that complicates communication between teenage youth and their middle-aged parents can be traced to the presence of two games going on simultaneously in the same house. Mom and Dad want to play PREPARING FOR LIFE. Study hard and you will get into college. Keep your room straightened up so that you will acquire the habit of neatness. Be regular. Get home on time. It will make you a steady, reliable, well-ordered adult.

So it will. But that's not everybody's game. Some girls want to play POPULARITY QUEEN, and the stakes are out there where the kids are, not at home in the messed-up bedroom. Some boys would rather play HOTROD or MAD SCIENTIST. Boys and girls alike may want to play WHO AM I? or LIVING FOR TODAY or any of the other games that the young can find so fascinating. It is simply no use for Mom and Dad to prove, patiently and conclusively, that what you do today affects what you will be twenty years from now. That is a different game, and we're not play-ing that one right now, thank you.

Theologians have been trying for a long time to relate Christian ethics to the world of business, and it hasn't been easy. Their first try was to bring the categories of personal morality into their analysis of behavior in the business world. The businessman was expected to play their game, call it GOOD SAM. Of course, it didn't work. As any honest businessman will tell you, when he is in his office, he doesn't play GOOD SAM. He might be a fine, lov-able Christian gentleman, devoted to his wife and chil-dren, loyal to his friends, and kind to dumb animals. But on the job, he's involved in a game called STAY AFLOAT, and he plays it for keeps. It's the only way.

Likewise, most of the common labor-management dis-putes can be understood as a result of too many games going on in the same shop at the same time. Production workers play STRETCHOUT, a simple game in which the worker tries to avoid working himself out of a job. Management has its own game, SPEEDUP, which has precisely the opposite goal: to get as much work out in as little time and at as little cost as possible. What's worse, management gets to hire the umpires: time-study men and industrial engineers.

The trouble here is not that labor and management do not understand each other. The trouble is that they understand each other only too well. No amount of verbiage about bigger pies for everybody can change the fact that two games which have opposite goals and contradictory rules are inevitably going to produce some interesting rhubarbs.

The issue of cheating in college can best be understood as a collision of games. The academic cheat subverts the fundamental basis of academic life, the saying goes, because he betrays the search for truth, which is the common ground of all scientific and humane learning. That's true, of course, but it is also true that the university, in addition to its official commitment to the game SEARCH FOR TRUTH also plays a game called DRIVER'S LICENSE. Anyone who wants to operate in our highly technical social order is required to produce, on demand, an operator's license called a degree.

Of course, everyone wants these degrees, and they will even work to get them—if they have to. So the university says, "All right, we'll give you a license. But first you have to play our game. Take these courses. Go to these classes. Spit out these responses on this paper, and we will give you points. Get enough points and you get your driver's license. If you get enough answers right, you get a free pass to another game called GRADUATE SCHOOL."

Is it any wonder that students have invented their own

game? Their game is very much like STRETCHOUT. It consists of getting the most points with the least work. GETTING THROUGH is the students' game. SEARCH FOR TRUTH is the professors' game. There is also a game called IMPROVING THE WHOLE MAN, but that is played best by the public relations office.

If you ask Constituted Authority what constitutes cheating, you get your answer in terms of SEARCH FOR TRUTH. A student cheats when he gets a good grade without searching for truth. But then, if you ask the student, the real cheat is the rat who turned him in for innocently copying an answer. He wasn't playing the game.

In this world of multiplying games, we commonly accord honor and prestige to the virtuoso who is adept at playing several games at the same time. The businessman who can STAY AFLOAT while playing GOOD SAM is, indeed, a paragon of virtue in everyone's eyes. Likewise, the student who can play DRIVER'S LICENSE and make straight A's while playing SEARCH FOR TRUTH will win both the enthusiastic respect of his fellow students and the enthusiastic recommendations of his professors.

But let a man pursue one game so ardently that he patently fails at another, and the crowds will boo him while the moralists point their long, bony fingers at him. The businessman who refuses to play GOOD SAM may make out well in business, but he will be regarded, even by his friends, as a tightfisted skinflint who can't be trusted out of your sight. And everyone knows what Constituted Authority does with students who are caught transgressing the rules of SEARCH FOR TRUTH. It throws them out of the game. No truth, no license.

We know all this, of course, and because such things happen rather often, we are inclined to regard our age as an age of declining virtue. But look at it the other way. We are just as hard on the businessman who plays GOOD SAM so expertly that his business goes under. And what would our professional searchers-for-truth do with a really energetic and dedicated searcher-for-truth who got so caught up in that game that he forgot to play DRIVER'S LICENSE at all? Well, he might find truth, but he wouldn't get his license. Then no one would recognize him as having any truth at all. And the last state of that man would, as the saying goes, be worse than the first.

So, you see, we do live by rules. And the great problem of the age is not that morals are deteriorating. It is that we have too many rules, too many games going on all at once. While you are busy keeping the rules of this game, you are being penalized for being out of bounds in that game over there.

What does this have to do with morality? Karl Marx gave us an interesting clue to the relationship when he pointed out that morality was whatever the ruling class decided would be in their own interest. In his view the bourgeois decided that thrift was a virtue because they needed to promote the accumulation of capital. They developed the idea of the sanctity of contract to protect their own business deals. They attacked the evils of drink because workers who drank reduced the efficiency of the industrial plant.

You don't have to be a Marxist to see the validity in this perception. The best I ever heard it stated was in a recent comic strip, "The Wizard of Id." The King was finishing up a speech with the exhortation, "And let us all remember to live by the Golden Rule." Someone asked the Wizard what was the Golden Rule, and he answered: "The one who has the gold makes the rule."

Now if this sounds a little cynical, let us all remember what Dr. Berne said about games. He pointed out that people play games for some ulterior purpose. They profit from playing the game in some way or other. And behold, when we look into the games we've been discussing, we find that here, too, people keep rules in game fashion in order to serve their own interest. Marx's point is that, having adopted the game as our own, we elevate it into a morality. We treat the person who breaks the rules of our game as a moral offender.

In the case of the student who cheats on examinations, the moral judgment of the academic community is clear: he has done wrong and he must suffer. That's quick, easy, and routine. Constituted Authority does not ask what it might have done to make possible, or even to encourage the offense. Questions like that are not part of the game. And on the other hand the student is likely to regard a fellow student who reports an incident of cheating with the same moral condemnation as that visited by the institution upon the cheater himself.

There is no doubt that the university punishes cheating as an act of self-protection. And there is no doubt that students punish talebearers for the same reason. So both games have been elevated to the status of moralities, and in both cases the offender is treated with righteous indignation.

This same confusion between games and morality explains why the convicted criminal often betrays a sense of righteous indignation when he is caught. His indignation may be directed against an informer, or against the police, who will sometimes take unfair advantage of an honest thief, or against the lawyer who has let him down. His resentment is based on his feeling that somebody didn't play the game.

In this world of games and gamesmanship, where does morality lie? I do not think it lies in preferring this game to that game, but rather lies beyond the games, beyond the world of rules and scorekeeping. For if this analysis has any validity, the rules themselves are often only elaborate self-justifications for things that we want to do in our own interest. In this moral supermarket you can pick out any brand that suits your taste at the moment.

If this is so, then the job of the moralist is not to announce the rules, obviously, because you can do that only if you are playing one of the games. His job is not to tell people how they ought to run their lives—that has never been the moralist's job. His job is pretty much what Dr. Berne sees as his job: to help people to see the game for what it is and maybe to throw little wrenches into the works so that the game gets fouled up.

When the game is exposed for what it really is, it becomes rather hard to play it with any great seriousness. At that point the genuine moral questions can be raised —the question of ultimate ethical commitments and the question of men's fundamental attitudes toward other people. Deprived of the subterfuge of his game, a man may be inspired to try to deal with reality in a responsible way. When the moralist is able to lead people into making this shift, he has done his work well.

There is nothing new about the morality game. People have always tried to find rules that would solve all their ethical problems. They have always used rules to free them from having to make hard choices. They have used the same rules as clubs with which to beat their neighbors. People have never been satisfied with moralists who refuse to play the game. That may be why genuine moralists have been so unpopular in every age.

9

Labor's Love Lost

THE past few years have seen a growing conversation about the hazardous future of work. All
sorts of people are concerned about the problem: economists, sociologists, psychologists, and even
theologians. What constitutes the problem is that our
industrial capacity has been growing larger year by year
while the number of production jobs declines.

The reasons are simple enough. We are developing
machines that can work pretty well by themselves. Cy-
bernetics and automation have combined to produce
"cybernation," which promises to create whole factories
that will be able to produce goods without the need for
people at all.

Imagine what that might mean. An automobile fac-
tory might consist of acres of automatic machines, work-

ing in response to directions supplied by a computer. Should a machine break down, the computer would receive a call for help and would respond through a set of taped instructions to another machine. Self-operating machines would be repaired and replaced automatically. Pretty neat! Who needs people? The time will come when a mere handful of very highly skilled workers will be able to produce enough of everything for everybody. We will all be rolling in affluence such as we have never known.

But the gratification of the seers over the prospect of unlimited affluence is coupled with alarm over the disappearance of work. If there are no jobs for people, how will they be able to buy in to the new affluence? Besides, can we really stand leisure? We have been culturally conditioned to a social doctrine of justification by work. How can we ever repudiate that heritage? Won't we get bored and stagnate? Or even more seriously, might we not turn to irrational acts of violence in an effort to relieve our boredom?

In the view of many observers of our future, we will have to learn how to love leisure and/or we will have to find moral equivalents for work, just as William James once counseled us to seek a moral equivalent for war. Since we have done so poorly in our search for the latter, we might well wonder if we will ever discover the former.

With respect to the question of leisure, I am not at all willing to take the Puritan work ethic as the last word. I prefer the old-fashioned view of Genesis that work is a curse and a punishment. Maybe we could argue that man has served his time and earned his release by virtue of his inventiveness. Work may have its redeeming qualities but there is no need to make it into a major virtue, as many of us Protestant-types have done.

I find myself attracted by the speculations of the new prophets of leisure, people like Herbert Marcuse and Norman O. Brown. They insist that the doctrine of work is destructive and unnecessary—a "surplus-repression" as Marcuse calls it—and we can well do without it. The prophets of leisure deplore the rationalization of life that the industrial age has produced. They tell us that rather than trying to control the world, we ought to sit back and enjoy it. In their view much of our labor is unnecessary. It is really made work. If we can learn to live without the necessity for work, we can accept the loss of work and begin to enjoy life for the first time.

You can't quarrel with that analysis. Certainly our experience with retired people shows that those who most enjoy retirement are people who have learned to not work. Compulsive workers soon get bored with retirement. They feel so useless and unhappy that many of them simply curl up and die. Even today we have a crying need to teach people to transcend the Puritan ethic against the day when man's work is done.

At the same time, leisure and work are not polar opposites. We usually think of work as strenuous and unpleasant exertion, while leisure means sitting around under a leafy tree while somebody serves up the mint juleps. Not so. Many of the things we do for fun make more demands upon us than does our professional work.

Suppose you like to garden. You do not have to do it, so it isn't really work. But once you decide to do it, then you must commit yourself to a certain amount of time and labor. There are certain things that have to be done just right or you won't have much of a garden. If you fail to spray, the bugs may get your plants. If you fail to weed, your garden will become overgrown. Your garden will impinge upon you in ways you will not always be able to foresee. The weeds will not grow in conformity with your vacation schedule. The insects will not put off their visits until you have time to deal with them.

For some years I have been spending the summers in a cottage colony inhabited by businessmen, professional men, and skilled workers. I have always been impressed with how hard many of these men work in their spare time. They always seem to be building something—an addition to the cottage, a dock, a concrete walk, a boat. They make repairs and renovations; they keep up their lawns and their gardens; they dig, paint, haul stone, and mix concrete. I am not convinced that this is merely a manifestation of the compulsive Puritan work ethic. They do these things because they really enjoy doing them—it is a form of play.

Perhaps this sort of playful work has promise in a world which is running out of compulsive work. But at the same time it is clear that even in the most advanced cybernated economy, there will always be some work that will have to be done. Someone has to keep all those machines going. Somebody—a lot of somebodies—will have to provide the myriads of personal services that the new affluence will surely demand. There will always be need for people with skill and imagination to design the systems that sustain the cybernated society, and those systems are likely to become more and more complex as time goes on.

This work may not keep everyone busy, but it will keep some people very, very busy. And while it may not be hard physical work, it will be very exacting work.

There will be no room for easy-going and relaxed attitudes toward the job, because everything will have to be done just right.

Nor will it be possible to repudiate the rationalization of the social order. A society that contains airlines and sewerage systems is always going to be rationalized to the very core, and there is nothing much we can do about that. When you fly in the airplane of the future, you may be quite unconcerned whether the pilot has to fly only once a month, but you don't want him to adopt a playful attitude toward all those gadgets he has to work in order to land the plane safely. In other words you will want him to do his work with rational precision. Otherwise you would probably prefer to walk.

In sum, we have to learn to value leisure and to stop being compulsive about work. But at the same time we cannot afford to devalue work. There is still too much important work to be done.

Now the leisuremongers say that it is a mistake to look for work just to give people something to do. They are right—up to a point. But then people seldom agree as to what constitutes made work. If we stop looking at American society as a closed system, we will find quite a few things that need to be done. The rest of the world has not quite caught up with our affluence. Maybe we ought to think about doing something in that direction before we lie back in our garden of Eden to enjoy the fruits of our nonlabor. That little project could easily keep us busy for several generations.

Even here at home there are plenty of jobs to be done. Most of our professions are open-end occupations. They can absorb as many people as can be spared to enter them—provided money is available to pay them. We could gear up education to the point where the whole nation could employ itself in teaching one other. The church alone could use ten times as many professional workers as it now has. There is work to be done if the people and the financial support are available.

But these are all functions that require a high degree of intelligence, education, and skill. What about those who are really in trouble: the average minds, the partially educated, the relatively unskilled? I am not sure we have to settle for the educational system we now enjoy. Maybe one day we will begin to learn how even people whom we now regard as mediocre can be developed into highly skilled professionals. But in the meantime let us concede that there are many people who are uneducated and unskilled and who prefer to stay that way. Could there be jobs for them?

Judging from the looks of our cities, I suspect we could keep a huge work force busy indefinitely just picking up papers, sweeping the streets, and keeping buildings and bridges clean. We don't even make the beginning of an honest effort to do this sort of thing today, simply because it costs too much. But if our resources were as close to being unlimited as some of our technological prophets now predict, I see no reason why a job of this character could not be offered to any citizen as a matter of right. You could work him, say, twenty hours a week in return for a full and adequate wage.

This need not be seen as a concession to the Puritan ethic. It would be a socially useful—even a necessary—project. We've become so used to looking at grime and litter in our cities that we hardly notice it anymore. Most of us take it for granted that cities have to be shabby and dirty. If we had the manpower and the resources, we could turn them into places of genuine gaiety and charm.

If we ever did manage to develop this kind of job, it might become highly popular with some very unlikely people, particularly with intellectuals. When you are in a position in which the results of your labor never show, when you never really know whether or not you are doing a decent job, you can appreciate the attractiveness of a job in which you can look back at the end of the day and see a clean street instead of the dirty one that was there in the morning. And if you had to work only twenty hours a week for your full dinner pail, you would have plenty of time left over for those intellectual and aesthetic pursuits for which professional man has so little time.

Why, you can even envision scholars, artists, and writers supporting themselves with honest toil which would enable them to escape the rat race of modern university life. Just think: no classes, no personal problems, no committee work. You would grade no papers—you would merely crumple them up and throw them into the ash can. What aesthetic satisfaction! Shades of Jefferson and Rousseau!

Then there are whole areas of society where the promise of a workless world never reaches. You may notice that most of the writers who are concerned with the disappearance of work turn out to be men. They have very little to say to women. In fact, they have not considered women at all. My wife pointed out to me this little gap in the affluent-unemployment thesis. "What about housekeeping?" she asked. Ah yes, what about housekeeping, indeed?

Maybe our houses will be fully automated someday, but there are few signs of it so far. To be sure, we have appliance upon appliance, but most appliances merely change the work from one form to another. In the old days, a woman did her washing on one day each week, and it usually took her all day. Now she just puts it into the automatic washer and then transfers it to the dryer. How easy. But the joke is that today she does a lot more washing. Her standard of cleanliness is much higher than it would have been two generations ago—clean clothes every day, no less. So the housewife washes oftener, and she washes far more clothes. I would bet that if you did a time-and-motion study of the daily routine of a modern housewife and compared it with that of her grandmother, you would find that she spends as many hours a week with the laundry as grandmother ever did.

It is the same with everything the housewife does. Give her a better vacuum cleaner, she does more cleaning. Automatic dishwasher—more dishes. She has a broiler, a toaster, a blender, and a mixer so she does more broiling, toasting, blending, and mixing than she would have done without the gadgets.

Moreover, large areas of housekeeping seem impervious to the inroads of mechanization, much less automation. Bedmaking is rather primitive, in spite of contour sheets. Laundry is sorted in much the same way it was done a century ago. We have many pre-prepared foods, but it's still a chore to put the food away after a shopping trip. Cooking itself continues to be a very time consuming job. And so far as I know, no one has yet succeeded in developing a method for changing diapers automatically, or for wiping runny noses, or for settling fights among the kids.

Automation has not yet begun to invade the household, and I wonder whether it is ever likely to do so. Housewifely routines have changed dramatically over the past fifty years, but homemaking is still a full-time job for most women. In the future they will very likely be working harder than their automated husbands.

You can argue that in the automated age every housewife will be able to afford a maid. But in the automated age I doubt whether anyone is going to want to be a maid. In any case it is no solution to the labor problem to get someone else to do the work. Work is still being done, whether by a maid for pay, or by a wife for free.

The housewife's only benefit from automation is likely to be an indirect one. With his twenty or thirty-hour work week, daddy may be around a lot more to help with the housework. Though this may come as good news to mother, I doubt that father will regard it in the same way. In fact, we will probably find him hiding out in his comfortable office every chance he gets.

We are hardly in danger of running out of work. Certainly, factory-type employment is declining, and the nation faces a massive task in reabsorbing displaced workers into the economic system. Certainly, too, we need to find ways to make resources available to pay unskilled people for unskilled work that is socially useful. Oddly enough our problem today is not that we are so affluent, but that we are apparently not affluent enough to finance all of the possible projects. If that is true, then it will be a long time before we even begin to approach the point at which we will be too rich to allow people to work.

But meanwhile, we do have a fair amount of leisure. Since we do, we ought to be listening carefully to the subversive voices that tell us to enjoy, enjoy. We have been far too moral about work. It is about time we

changed our tune and began to see work once more as
the Bible sees it: realistically and without sentimentality.
It is a regrettable necessity which we must endure because of the nature of the world we live in. When we
finally absorb that message, we won't necessarily stop
working, but we may begin to relax about it. Hard work
won't hurt anyone—so long as he doesn't let it become a
religion.

10

Blast-off to Nowheresville

I HAD a curious experience a few months ago. At least it seems curious as I think about it now. I was turning on the TV set for my youngest TV watcher when I stumbled onto the telecast of a launching at Cape Kennedy. I watched the rocket take off, mildly interested. My boy wasn't even interested. He was mad at the space agency because his favorite cartoon show had been canceled.

Only later did it occur to me to ask someone what I had seen. Sure enough, what I had seen was a Significant Step in the American Space Program. Two men, Pete Conrad and Richard Gordon, had been sent into orbit, one of them to walk around a bit at the end of his tether. Like all good American travelers, they sent back some fine color shots of the scenery. The mission was a

Success, and we were all assured that we are, indeed, far ahead of the Russians. And that was that.

What a far cry from just a few years ago when Colonel Glenn made the first American orbit and brought us within hailing distance of the Russians. Glenn rated trips to the White House (which have become standard operating procedure, I understand) and ticker-tape parades (which have not), and his name was on everyone's lips. But most of Glenn's successors quickly passed into anonymity so far as the public is concerned.

I wonder what it all means. A multimillion dollar, epoch-making project enacted before our very eyes, and our response is, "What do they mean, taking my favorite show off TV for this?" I suspect that this response represents the final failure of our scientific game, CAN YOU TOP THIS? We are all impressed with the fantastic achievements of science in our century. But that is just the trouble. The scientists have convinced us that they can do anything. So what's new? Why should we be surprised when they actually do it? It has been a long time since I have met anyone who seriously doubted that we could put a man on the moon if we choose to do so. Most of us would be far more surprised if we failed.

But how strange it is. As the skepticism about the claims of science has faded, the glamor of science has faded, too. Many people are now beginning to raise questions about the future of the scientific enterprise. Time was when whatever science wanted was fine by everyone. The expanding frontiers of knowledge had to be pushed out. If you questioned this goal, you were put into the category of those who once thought the world was flat. How about Columbus? Suppose he had had that attitude? Where would we all be today?

That argument used to be enough to put anyone on the defensive. But not anymore. People have begun to wonder about the unqualified benevolence of the scientific establishment. Certainly the A-bomb had something to do with the change in attitude. You could justify our development of the A-bomb on the ground that if we hadn't done it, the Germans would have. Yes, but there were German scientists, too. Being a scientist evidently does not guarantee that you will always be on the side of truth and right.

But there is more to the new attitude than mere mistrust of the scientist. People are beginning to realize that though science can do anything, it cannot do everything. Science is no longer carried on by solitary figures working in their basements. It is carried on by well-paid professionals in modern, up-to-date surroundings, using a lot of very expensive equipment and materials. Science costs money, and that is why it cannot do everything. Someone has to decide who is to get the scientific dollar, to put it crudely.

How do we decide where the money is to go? We are just beginning to raise that question. What about the moon race, anyway? Is there any earthly use in landing a man—or a lot of men—on the moon? Up to now, it has been easy. If you were to ask, "Why go to the moon?" they would just answer, "Because it's there." Of course, that is just as good an argument for not going.

The "because it's there" argument may be fine as a justification for climbing Mount Everest—it is a leisured sportsman's sort of reason. After all the mountain climber presumably climbs on his own money and on his own time. At least he costs me nothing. But going to the moon—that is my money and I cannot for the life of me see the faintest bit of rational sense in it.

How about the Columbus argument? Let's remember that contrary to popular belief Columbus did not set sail for the Indies to prove that the world was round. He knew that already. He was nobody's fool. Of course, the Queen of Spain and her knuckle-headed advisers did not know it—they shared the popular prejudices of the day. The Queen was taking a real chance.

But the Queen was not doing it for science or for adventure. Neither was Columbus, for that matter. The two of them were able to do business together because they were after the same thing: money. Columbus figured that he had a shortcut to the Indies. He could escape the pirates and the Arabs and beat out the Portuguese at the same time. Columbus was looking for trade, and he had no doubt about the economic consequences of his voyage. Now that sort of motive I can understand.

As it turned out, Columbus was all wrong, as every schoolboy knows. But he did discover something important, so it all came out all right. And this, say the science boosters, is the Great Lesson. You set out to do something, and you end up doing something else, often something far more valuable. In failing to reach one goal, you attain some other goal that you never even anticipated. So let's send our man to the moon. Who knows what important by-products we may discover.

Maybe so. I remember reading one impressively learned article that justified the entire space program on the ground that it had taught us invaluable lessons about the management of incredibly complex and precise enterprises. It was a very convincing argument which could be used to justify any useless project that anyone could possibly think up. It falls into the same category as the adage that no man is totally useless. He can always serve as a bad example.

In spite of the apparent uselessness of the project, the moon race is clearly in the cards to stay. Barring all other persuasions, its final justification will no doubt be National Defense. The invocation of that potent phrase is enough to end all argument. Quiet descends and we all kneel while the acolyte puts out the candles. Nobody knows just what the moon race is defending, but then you never can tell . . .

The old prestige argument is just as spooky. According to this view, we have to win the race to the moon so that the rest of the world will be convinced that we have not lost our starch, as the Communists have been predicting. Then all the nations of the earth will remain our loyal friends and allies. Again, you cannot argue with this one. You either swallow it or you don't. My only regret is that we have to find such distressingly unscientific supports for our great leap into space.

I have always conceived of the space program, rather naïvely, as a very high level WPA project for engineers and technicians. I have no objections to that. I just think we might be able to dream up more useful WPA projects. If the President should care to ask, I have a little list. Meanwhile, I really begrudge the scientists that thirty-five billion dollars that they are shooting off into the ethereal realm. The scientists used to accuse theological types of being too otherworldly and of not paying enough attention to the ills of mankind right here on earth. Seems like the tide has turned.

Next to the incredibly significant project of landing a man on the moon is the almost equally significant project of designing a two-thousand-mile-per-hour supersonic jetliner. The price tag for this little enterprise will be about three billion, give or take a billion. The supersonic jetliner can't do any major harm, except for sending a shock wave over a twenty-mile area on either side of its course. I am sure we will get used to that in time.

Of course, there will be other little disadvantages. We are only beginning to learn something about the effects of drastic changes in the time schedule upon the human mind and body. A supersonic plane will make those time shocks far more severe, perhaps so severe that adjustment to the time change will pose far greater problems for the traveler than getting there a few hours later.

But don't worry about that. We can always dig up another billion or two that will enable us to investigate the causes of the adjustment problem. In twenty years or so we will no doubt have it licked. Meanwhile, take another tranquilizer. They're on the house.

These promised giants of the airways have more mundane problems connected with them. As every air traveler has learned, suitcases really know how to live. They never hurry for anyone. If you have ever had the good fortune to wait at an airport while your luggage arrives at the baggage room in its own leisurely fashion, you can just imagine the thrill and excitement of waiting after one of these supersonic jobs lands and disgorges seven to nine hundred passengers, complete with luggage for an overseas trip. Every baggage room will look like Lincoln Center at intermission time.

Now don't get me wrong. I am not against progress. I just want to be sure that it is really progress before I buy it. And when I spend that kind of money, I want something for it, something which I know is worth the money. These ephemeral, theoretical benefits leave me cold. Whatever happened to that good old-fashioned American pragmatic, utilitarian, show-me attitude?

For example, I am sure that every air traveler would agree that the next great breakthrough in air transportation will be not greater speed in the air, but greater speed on the ground. Most travelers would be quite happy if their speedy jet could land them at their downtown hotel without need for airport limousines, helicopter flights, or expensive cabs. Why not spend a couple of those billions on designing vertical-lift planes that could take off from and land on the roof of a downtown building?

Just think: you could roar through the air at six hundred miles an hour, come to a screeching halt over downtown Manhattan, and descend quietly and precisely to the plane-sized parking space on a roof, or in a lot, or in some special terminal arrangement. You could go quickly downstairs or underground to a waiting vehicle or walkway and be where you want to go in no time at all. Now there is a useful project. It could really do something for air travel.

This kind of experiment is already under way, of course. The military have for several years been developing all sorts of sophisticated helicopters for use in Vietnam. Chances are that their efforts will bear fruit in time, and all travelers will be the beneficiaries.

You can hardly quarrel with that analysis. Only it seems too bad that we civilians have to take our technological advances like droppings from the mouth of the war machine. Could we not spend money to do this sort of thing because it is useful and worthwhile, not just because it might give us some military advantage in some war or other?

Then we might develop such handy little inventions as the electric car. There are plenty of good commercial reasons why some people do not want to see an electric car developed. But if cars really do contribute substantially to the creation of smog, then perhaps we ought to develop the electric car no matter whose business suffers. I note that one of our major automobile companies has, in fact, developed an experimental electric car, but that design still has a long way to go. I cannot conceive of the possibility that a society which can send a man to the moon could not produce an automobile that will run quietly without smogging up the landscape.

Well, we all have our pet projects, just as we all have our pet hates. I am not rabid about the moon bit, you understand. It makes jobs. It produces a little excitement. But it does seem curious that Americans—the fastest-dealing, sharpest-trading, toughest and most practical people in the whole wide world—have suddenly become dewy-eyed and almost mystical about what turns out to be a gloriously romantic and amazingly intricate game. But then we have always been suckers for games. And in spite of our well-advertised preference for the underdog, we really do like to be on the winning side.

So I am sure we will go to the moon. And I am sure we will get there first. I hope so. Maybe then we will find something really useful for all those unemployed scientists and technicians to do with themselves. If they have trouble finding anything, I'll still have that little list.

11

A Surfeit of Symbols:

The Age of Mystification in the Theater

IT all started with *The Cocktail Party*. Well no, it didn't really start then. People have always dissected plays in an attempt to understand what the writer *really* means. They have been doing it with Shakespeare for centuries with only indifferent success.

But a whole new era opened up with the production of T. S. Eliot's first postwar play back in 1949. So many elements in the play seemed to demand explanation that it was impossible to take the work at face value. A highly unlikely psychiatrist acted as a *deus ex machina*. An improbable sequence of events included a vast conspiracy to rearrange people's lives. The psychiatrist sent an attractive young woman on a way of negation that would lead, finally, to a horrible death on an anthill—by crucifixion, no less.

Who was this strange psychiatrist? Was he merely a clever manipulator? Or was he God? Were Julia and Alex merely a pair of opportunistic do-gooders? Or were they really a pair of guardian angels? Was the play trying to deal with psychiatry and contemporary values? Or was it really a profound religious tract disguised as a modern comedy of manners?

The critics had fun puzzling over these questions and so did the general public. *The Cocktail Party* became the leading topic of conversation at numerous cocktail parties throughout the land, until James Thurber provided a *coup de grâce* with his delightful New Yorker piece, "What Cocktail Party?" After that, it was difficult to take the discussion very seriously any more.

But the furor over *The Cocktail Party* opened up a whole new realm of possibilities for the playwright, and the crafty ones lost no time in exploiting the territory. Symbolism became fashionable, *de rigeur*, as they say. Dramatists, of course, have always dealt with symbols. They are a primary means of establishing contact with an audience. But seldom in the past has symbolism been so self-conscious, contrived, and overworked.

I once heard the late Flannery O'Connor remark that she had recently been asked by a college student how she went about writing her novels. "Do you start with the symbols and weave the story around them?" the student asked. "Or do you write the story first and put the symbols in afterward?" The casual observer might suspect that some of our contemporary playwrights have been doing a little of both. So the public wants to hunt for symbolic references in a play? Very well, we will provide material for their guessing games.

I am not sure what Mr. Eliot was up to in *The Cocktail Party*. I am willing, on the whole, to accept the conventional explanation that he was interested in affirming the traditional Christian interpretation of life—both the Way of Affirmation and the Way of Negation. According to this view, Eliot resorted to the indirections of *The Cocktail Party* as a way of getting a hearing. He knew the modern playgoing public would readily accept a cocktail party as a dramatic device. He knew, likewise, that a contemporary audience would accept the psychiatrist in the role of high priest, because that is precisely how society regards the psychiatrist anyway. Sir Henry, then, becomes not so much a genuine, believable psychiatrist as a spokesman for the Christian way. Thus, his lapses of professional decorum—not to say simple manners—are not to be regarded too seriously.

After the success of *The Cocktail Party*, unbridled symbolism galloped all over the contemporary stage and even spilled out onto the movie screen. Sometimes it was the psychiatric symbolism of Freudian depth psychology. At other times it was the symbolic heritage of Christendom, usually misused and frequently abused. What the symbols were supposed to symbolize was not always clear. But that only added zest to the game, and people continued to go to plays in order to become baffled about what the playwright "really means."

Tennessee Williams has been the leading perpetrator of Freudian symbolism in the present generation. *A Streetcar Named Desire* fairly reeks with it. Poor Blanche

Dubois is portrayed as a nervous bundle of libidinous energy, a fact which is underscored by her sneaky but heavy drinking, her fear of strong lights, and her frequent hot baths.

Williams pays a great deal of attention to names, using them as pointers, often in a rather heavy-handed manner. The streetcar that is named Desire takes you to one called Cemeteries, which, in turn, takes you to Elysian Fields. Blanche herself: white girl—for purity, of course. Stella—for star. The excessively spiritual young lady in *Summer and Smoke* is named Alma, which, as she carefully points out, is Spanish for soul.

Well so far, so good. Nothing especially complicated about that. Stella for star turns out to be more earthy than ethereal, while Blanche for purity turns out to be considerably less than pure. Alma spends her play discovering her own physicality—too late, of course. A fine sense of irony which the innocent symbolism of names only underscores.

But Williams is less successful with his excursions into Christian symbolism. The cannibalism of *Suddenly Last Summer* may be intended as a sacrilegious version of the Eucharist, though I am not sure about that. In any case it is of little importance. Many modern writers like to play around with black masses. It is a harmless pursuit but a little meaningless since most Americans haven't the faintest conception of what constitutes a mass of any color.

It is in his ill-fated *The Milk Train Doesn't Stop Here Anymore* that Williams's clumsy attempts at symbolism become disastrous. *Milk Train* is the story of an aging beauty—a Tennessee Williams stand-by—who is living in a magnificent villa on an island in the Mediterranean while steadfastly refusing to face the fact that she is dying. To her island comes a gorgeous young man who apparently makes a practice of dropping in on rich, elderly ladies about to expire, a practice which has earned him the name "The Angel of Death."

This young man is about thirty-five. He is blond and bearded. He possesses remarkable strength. He writes poetry and speaks words of undeniable, if unintelligible, profundity. His name, of course, is Christopher. Get it? Sound like anyone you know?

Just what this tale is all about is not quite clear. The lady expires in due course, and the gentleman takes some credit for having helped her face her last moments, though the script leaves some doubt as to how much help he really was. Then he and the old lady's female secretary chummily share a goblet of wine before sitting down to a sumptuous meal on the terrace as the curtain falls.

The thinly disguised Christ figure functions only as a foil against which we can see the lady's anger and frustration as she faces the certainty of approaching death. He adds nothing significant to the plot. If he is, indeed, intended to be a Christ figure, then the playwright has a very weird view of just what constitutes a Christ. On the other hand, Christopher may be only a very elaborate plant who serves to leave the critics perplexed and the playwright doubled up with derisive laughter.

I rather think that this has happened over and over again in some of our most successful drama. The passion for symbol searching has reached such proportions that the playwrights are tempted to put them in here and there, where they function not as symbols at all, but as theatrical booby traps to seduce the unwary and lead him off into irrelevancies.

Edward Albee has become another symbolic-booby-trap artist in recent years. In his earlier plays he would take the revered stereotypes of American culture and poke good, clean, vicious fun at them. In so doing he led many of us to suspect that he would one day emerge as a major playwright. But then, Albee got symbol happy, and the results have not been encouraging.

Take *Who's Afraid of Virginia Woolf?* for example. *Virginia Woolf* is a first-rate play, but it would be even better if it were not cluttered up with irrelevant symbols. I recently read a sober review of the movie version which proclaimed that the whole meaning of the work hangs on the identification of George and Martha as— you guessed it—General and Mrs. Washington. Their imaginary child is the lost American dream, for they cannot face the fact that it is unreal. American woman is loud, coarse, and bitchy, and American man is weak, bewildered, and ineffectual.

Well now, if that is what Albee had wanted to say, he could have said it all without writing a play. And if that is what he really meant to say in this play, then we would have to write him off as a pretentious ass. But I do not think that Albee is that phony, nor do I think that he meant to say anything of the sort. He wrote a simple, straightforward play about four people who are anything but simple and/or straightforward. But in so doing he fell into the symbolizing trap of naming the chief characters George and Martha—not accidentally, but with the juvenile prankster's delight in fooling the stuffy world of critics and symbolmongers.

Virginia Woolf's name in the title, as a playful parody

on "Who's Afraid of the Big Bad Wolf" is delightful and suggestive at the same time. But if it is meant to be an obscure reference to the real Virginia Woolf, who also wrote in English, who had her own fantasy world, and who committed suicide, etc., then I would have to object that this has very little to do with anything—especially the play. Nor would I blame Albee himself for this bit of symbol prospecting. It is the critics who have been tempted to make illusory mountains out of allusory molehills.

But Albee does become a symbolmonger of the first degree in *Tiny Alice*. Here is a play that seems profound until you begin to think about it. Then you realize that it has not said or done anything at all. It diddles with reality without ever making a statement about it, except for some conventional things such as: "Princes of the Church are corrupt and venal" and "Innocent young men are rather easy for a good-looking girl to seduce."

The play does no more than play around with symbolic material. The question of what is real and what is unreal is one that men have puzzled over for as long as they have been puzzling. Albee, unfortunately, fails to carry the conversation further.

As the play closes, the stage is filled with what we are told is "the shadow of a great presence," which overwhelms the dying Julian, the young lay brother who has presumably been corrupted and destroyed—or is it redeemed? The shadow is the presence of—God? Alice? Or are they both the same? It wonders one. But not very much.

Julian, of course, dies in a posture of crucifixion. I am not sure why this should be so, except that it marks the play as being undeniably religious, for, after all, is not crucifixion a very religious way to die? We are, happily, not told that Julian is thirty-three years old, though it would not make much difference if he were.

Tiny Alice is not a very bad play. It does have convincing characterizations and some brilliant dialogue. But it is not about anything. The routine manipulation of symbolic devices and murky allusions is no substitute for an idea. Unfortunately the theatergoing public has learned the symbols game well enough to enable a play like *Tiny Alice* to get itself taken seriously even though it has little substance to it.

In the world of motion pictures, Ingmar Bergman has done much of the same sort of playing around with symbols. *The Virgin Spring* retells a traditional miracle story about the rape-murder of a young girl, her father's slaughter of the killers, and the eruption of a miraculous spring of water on the site of the murder. The film closes with the father's announcement that on this spot he will build a church.

The story itself is simple, almost to the point of being corny. But Bergman's stark realism makes it seem believable and important. At the same time he plays up the symbolic elements in the story. He devotes considerable footage to the father's careful and deliberate bathing before he goes into the hall to take his revenge upon the murderers. The bath is treated as a ritual act, making it seem more significant than a mere exercise in sanitation. It seems more like a rite of purification and preparation, very much like the Lavabo in the liturgy.

All this is perfectly respectable, though a little overdone. *The Seventh Seal* is more complicated. It is a symbolmonger's paradise, from the opening shot of a wheeling bird to the closing shot of the line of doomed plague victims marching up the hill to the castle of death.

The story concerns a gaunt and troubled knight who

is lured into playing a game of chess with death because he wants to know the meaning of it all. The knight's squire, a tough, ribald but compassionate skeptic is content to keep his belly full and never mind the metaphysical speculation. Through the course of the picture, the two acquire an assortment of hangers-on until the knight finally loses his chess game, and death comes to claim them all. Death explains that he, too, does not know the meaning of it all.

In the company there is a young juggler who has a beautiful wife and a fine baby boy. His name is Joseph and his wife's name is Mary. Begin to sound familiar? Unfortunately we are not given the name of the child. This little—I hesitate to say holy—family is spared the pains of death. There is no reason for this, of course. But we are led to see them as simple and ignorant. This Christ figure evidently stands for a very sentimental version of innocence.

Bergman's clumsy handling of symbolic material is at least partially redeemed by the sheer beauty of his finished product. He makes up in craftsmanship what he lacks in profundity. The viewer always leaves a Bergman work with the feeling that he has just seen something terribly important, but he is not sure just what. He has a sense of having missed the point and is likely to blame himself for his opaqueness. Perhaps someone else has the clue. But no one does. Not Bergman himself, surely.

I enjoyed *The Seventh Seal* and have gone back to see it again and again. I was most impressed not with its murky symbolism, but with its brutally realistic treatment of medieval life. The Age of Faith was, among other things, an age of coarseness, brutality, and exploitation. Nowhere else have I ever seen so convincing a treatment of this side of the Middle Ages. The symbolism was useful only in adding to the medieval atmosphere. It added nothing to the comprehension.

For myself, I rather prefer the straightforward way that Samuel Beckett uses symbolic material. Perhaps I am prejudiced because I think that *Waiting for Godot* is one of the great plays of our time. Like other contemporary playwrights, Beckett plays with religious symbols, quotes the New Testament, parrots theology, and introduces symbolic boobytraps. The tree, for example, that surprisingly sprouts a few tired leaves between acts —is it a symbol of hope, or is it merely illusory?

In a sense that tree provides a key to understanding the play. Beckett never says what the tree means. Though he uses symbols throughout—even the faded derby hats of the two tramps have a symbolic character —he never says, or even hints, what they might signify. Nor does he deny their significance. He does not know himself what they mean. When Beckett was asked what the play means, he is reported to have replied, "If I knew, I would have said so in the play."

This is what I mean when I call Beckett's use of symbol straightforward. Beckett says, "Look! Here are all these things. What do they mean? Do they mean anything?" The observer or the critic is invited to offer his own answers. Critic Martin Esslin says that the play is an exposition of the existentialist conviction that at the heart of reality is meaninglessness. For theologian Nathan Scott the play points to the characteristic of our age as a time of waiting for a new breakthrough of meaning. For Beckett, either may be right. He does not pretend to know.

The major difference between Beckett and, say, Albee is that although Beckett may not accept the traditional meanings associated with the symbols of Christian faith, he does know what meanings they have traditionally had. Therefore, he can use symbols intelligently; Albee cannot. To be a Christ figure a man must be more than just any thirty-three-year-old loser. Not every meal is a representation—or even an adequate parody—of the Eucharist. If a playwright is unable to assimilate the meanings which people actually attach to symbols, he had better forego their use entirely, unless he merely manages to make a fool of himself.

There is some hope that symbolmongering has about run its course. We live in an age that questions many of the old meanings and traditional forms of faith, so we have no grounds for complaint against the playwright who holds those meanings up to ridicule because he finds them empty. But we have a right to quarrel with the playwright who spreads symbolic-sounding allusions throughout his work in addition to, or as a substitute for, the meaning of the work itself.

Playgoers are beginning to act as though they feel the way I do. *Virginia Woolf* made it as realistic drama, and most audiences—both those who saw the play and those who saw the movie—were quite unconcerned about the resemblances of the names of the characters to actual persons, living or dead. In spite of some favorable critical notices, *Tiny Alice* turned out to be the flop it deserved to be—as *Milk Train* had been a short time earlier.

It's a good thing, too. Playwrights simply cannot turn out good drama when they get themselves tied up with foggy metaphysics and obscure symbolism. It is hard enough for a man to write well on the lines without having to fill up the space between the lines as well.

12

Cold Feet in the Promised Land:

*Some Second Thoughts
About Secularization*

Nor too long ago, "secular" was a bad word. Secularists were people who thought only on the flat planes of this world. They could neither ascend to the heights of the spirit nor plumb the depths of human existence. They were blind to the immense possibilities of man for good and for evil, because they had no sense of sin. Secularists were the real enemy because, no matter how much they resembled Christians on the outside, on the inside they were worlds apart because they had no God, you see.

But that's all changed. Now we're told that the secular world is not all bad. The emergence of a new attitude toward the secular world has been one of the most interesting developments in contemporary Christianity.

"Secular" means openness to the future, to new possibilities, to new forms of life and thought. Secularization
may mean the end of religion, but it's not opposed to
faith. It merely asserts the radical independence of this
world and its concerns.

Now the enemy is not the secular world but Christendom, the view that the religious institution belongs at
the center of society, its God somehow equated with
the shared values of that society. Christendom must go,
is going, has gone. The traditional forms of church life
and the culture-religion associated with Christendom
are to be repudiated in favor of a new secular aware-
ness, a new pragmatic openness to the new.

This newly emerging secular culture can best be
understood as a new climate in which the church has to
live and do its work. Christendom was, as it were, a
tropical climate. Whether you were inside the church
or outside, you hardly noticed the difference. Religious processions used to spill out of the church and into
the neighborhood and the surrounding countryside without anyone feeling the least bit self-conscious about it.
Priests used to go all over town in their cassocks, and
people accepted it as normal.

While the church was spilling out into the world, the
world was spilling into the church. Leading dignitaries
of the state and the professions occupied their places
in church on Sunday mornings as a part of their public
duty. Rich men celebrated their achievements by building churches or endowing chapels just as today they
give money to their alma mater.

But secularization has brought a sharp drop in the
cultural temperature. Today there are notable distinc-
tions between church and "not church." The parades

and processions have ceased. When they do occur, they impress you as being contrived and artificial. Today no sensible cleric would be caught dead walking down a busy street in his cassock. Many even feel a little self-conscious wearing a clerical collar to the theater. People keep turning around to look at them whenever somebody says something gamy—to get permission to laugh, I presume.

So the weather is colding up a bit. Bad weather for sitting around speculating, but good weather for Getting Things Done. Bracing weather, as they say. Good time to get off your butt and live.

Now let me make it clear that I'm all for this. I've been secular man all along, I begin to realize, and I'm just glad that people like Harvey Cox and Ronald Gregor Smith and Dennis Munby and Hans Hoekendijk have come along to tell me it's OK. I've never been able to get up much honest enthusiasm for family prayers or hymn sings or quiet days or blessing the house or the hounds or whatever. But at the same time, I'm not altogether ready to leave the campfire and go out into the cold night air. I'll moan and complain about the turgid, sluggish institution that insists on keeping one foot in the Middle Ages, but there are some things about it that I'll miss when they go. And there are some things about this exciting new secular order that I don't think I'm going to like.

For one thing I'm a little leery of this new pragmatic man that Harvey Cox sees as the ideal embodiment of urban-secular man. He's tough, confident, open, un-sentimental—when you put it that way, the picture isn't too reassuring. We're lulled a bit when we find he's really talking about John F. Kennedy.

But wait a minute! John F. Kennedy had one foot

in the Middle Ages if anybody did. Why, he even belonged to that irrelevant, otherworldly, medieval institution, the Roman Catholic Church—and before *aggiornamento*, too. And there's some evidence that Kennedy took his religion seriously, though he didn't wear it on his sleeve in the traditional American style. Maybe he was able to be tough and pragmatic and open to the future precisely because his roots were deep in the historic faith.

If we're looking for real historic models for secular, pragmatic man, we'd be more likely to come up with people like Jay Gould. Now there's a man who really fits the definition. He was practical—he certainly got things done. He wasn't soft or sentimental—he was hard to the point of ruthlessness. He was self-confident —he forged right ahead without any visible restraint. And pragmatic? Well, he wasn't deterred by any old-fashioned moral considerations, at any rate.

There are plenty of little Jay Goulds running around the secular city today. They run corrupt political machines. They exploit poor people. They pollute the air. They overcrowd the city with ugly but prosperous buildings. A few more of these tough and unsentimental pragmatic operators and the secular city is likely to blow sky-high.

The secular urbanizers are all pretty hard on traditional small-town values, particularly those that have to do with personal relationships. The impersonality of the city is not dehumanizing, they say. It frees us to be truly human by choice. Jane Jacobs, for example, has pointed out that the noninvolvement syndrome, notable among city dwellers, is not characteristically urban. It's a reaction of the ex-suburbanite against compulsive togetherness. If relating to other people is bound to lead to that smothering all-over-each-other-all-the-time total involvement, then those people plan to have nothing to do with nobody nohow. Being a true city dweller means you treat people with detachment and respect. You don't dialogue with the checker at the supermarket, and you don't I-thou with the man who takes tolls on the expressway.

I'm glad to hear that. I've never been able to make small talk with the service-station attendant while he puts gas in the car. I'm usually thinking about something else. And I've never been able to keep up with the chatter in the barber shop. I usually fall asleep in the chair. Now I don't have to feel guilty about it anymore. I'm in the urban style.

But hold on again. Doesn't this view of impersonality assume that every man has the chance to become a person sometime, somewhere? Many of us have that chance, of course, and we thrive in the city. What about those who don't? What about the people whose whole lives consist of external, impersonal I-you relationships? Could they be the lost and lonely people that the playwrights and novelists are writing about?

Personnel people in business and industry tell us that most of their employee problems stem from the unfulfilled human needs of the people working for them. When a functional business office has too many of these unmet needs, too many "yous" struggling to be "thous," all hell can break loose. It can get to be like trying to run a computer full of poltergeists.

No matter how urban we get to be, we're going to have to learn how to keep some of those small-town values around. We have to keep ourselves alive to the

humanity of the people around us unless we want to end
up being part-time people.

There are a lot of small-town characteristics that
manage to survive in the city. After living in my corner
of Washington, D.C., for four years, I find myself running into people I know whenever I go to a store in the
neighborhood, or even walk around the block. Whenever I work in the yard, there's always somebody driving
by who toots his horn and waves, or some neighbor
walks by with one of those dogs who apparently patrol
my block twenty-four hours a day.

At the risk of seeming like an alien influence in the
city, the church still has to preserve its historic role of
providing a milieu where people can be themselves. Of
course, the friendly-church bit has had it. Most people
in the city would rather, on the whole, be left alone. But
on the other hand there are all kinds of people. There are
those who need an arm to lean on, a shoulder to cry on,
a place where somebody knows them by name. Maybe
they are the modern-day equivalent of the biblical lame,
halt, and blind. No matter how urban the church becomes, it can't afford to lose its small-town concern for
the people who haven't made it in the city.

I have a few reservations about this *avant-garde*
church that seems to be in the cards for the secular age.
I gather that it's to be a group of really dedicated people
who have met the Lord, as the saying goes, people
who mean business and who are on fire with the call to
serve. To anybody who has had to wrestle with trying
to inject a little Christianity into the hopelessly bland little
clubs we call local churches, this prospect may seem
most attractive—but look out.

I've run into a few collections of such people in my

time and, I warn you, they have problems of their own. They are always deadly earnest and terribly serious. They display a kind of militant intensity that makes me want to flee to the comparatively easy going confines of the nearest monastery. They are always upset over the state of the world, and they are usually convinced that We Are to Blame.

Now a few people like this in the average nondescript congregation may be just what the doctor ordered. But a whole crew of them! Well, I would just rather not think about the prospect. The very thought leaves me quite exhausted.

By and large the secular theologians are pretty hard on the physical fabric of the church. Those elaborate and costly buildings often seem like so many millstones around the neck of ecclesiastical creativity. But I don't feel quite ready to abandon the church building. At the very least it's a visible sign of the presence of Christianity. For what it may be worth, I'm not at all sure that a skyline dominated by high-price high-rises is any more satisfying aesthetically than one dominated by church steeples.

We had a good example of this sort of shift here in Washington a short time ago. The National Presbyterian Church sold its magnificent old building (for a couple of million) and bugged out of downtown to build a fancy new building in a more cushy part of town. A number of civic groups (none of them church related) fought the move and tried to save the building, whose fine old tower had dominated that area of Connecticut Avenue. Now Connecticut Avenue looks a lot more secular, but I rather liked it the way it was. The church tower served as a visible symbol of the presence

of Christ in the city. The change would seem to symbolize one of the predominant facts of the secular
order: money talks.

But never fear, the Washington skyline is now capped
by the great tower of the Washington Cathedral. Now
there are a lot of arguments against the cathedral:
biblical—"it might have been sold for much and the
money given to the poor"(Matt. 26:9); aesthetic—
"It's phony Gothic"; economic—"It's an ecclesiastical
WPA"; theological—"It's the biggest golden calf in the
world."

Maybe—but still, it grabs you. As a symbol it may be
quite out of touch with our time. Its design may
be unoriginal, its art derivative, its usefulness as a place
of worship subverted by its medieval form. But when
you go inside, you can't escape the feeling it exudes of
the utter confidence and stability of the Christian faith.
The faith itself may be a little less solid than the Indi-
ana-limestone walls of the cathedral, but that's nothing
new. Even in the Middle Ages, cathedral building was
something of an act of defiance in the face of wars and
plagues and suffering that we can't even imagine today.
A world without cathedrals may be more rational, more
practical, and even more authentic, but I don't think it
would be a richer world for the change.

Here in Washington I've encountered one of the most
curious customs of the Age of Christendom to survive in
our time: the Methodist bus trip. Every year, dozens of
Methodist churches, mostly in the Midwest, get together a group of people, a busload or two, and come
to Washington. There they see the sights, visit the national shrines, visit their congressman, and tour the
shrines of Methodism. This phenomenon has been some-

thing totally new to me. I can't imagine an Episcopal church going to all that trouble. I'm not even clear as to why the Methodists do it. When you ask them, they invariably mumble something about "fellowship."

In the secular age, of course, this sort of thing will no doubt disappear. If you're going to Washington, why go with your fellow Methodists? Why not just mix with the secular world and go Greyhound? This business of going places with church groups is certainly an outmoded survival from the age of Christendom.

Of course, that's true, but I'll have to admit that I find the idea appealing. It does build upon and add to the solidarity of the parish community. And it might not be such a bad thing for some of those congressmen on the Hill to be reminded that the local Methodists have their eye on them. At the same time the Washington trip provides an opportunity for the Methodist social-action crowd and all the other bureaucratic intellectuals to get a crack at some of their people. All this may disappear as we become fully secularized, but I'll be sorry to see that happen.

Then there are all those banquets and meetings that seem to require the presence of a minister for invocations and blessings. I'm as tired of those things as the next man, and I get impatient with all of the *pro-forma* religious expressions that Christendom demands. But at the same time I must admit that many of my most useful excursions into the secular order have come out of encounters at such trivial affairs. If we get too neat and tidy about them, we'll find ourselves all barricaded up in an ecclesiastical bunker.

I'd have to say the same for many of the routine events that take place in the church. Our traditional antipathy toward those casual, marginal people who go to church merely to get hatched, matched, and dispatched may be due for a revision. It's no small thing for a man to concede that the church has something to say to him at moments like these, when he's really confronting the elemental issues of life. The trouble is that he usually gets shortchanged. The clergy grind him out a service as mechanically as they grind out programs on their mimeograph machines. They don't tell him what they're doing or why. They take him at face value and assume that he only wants meaningless motions. So everybody's opinion of everybody else is confirmed and strengthened. When Christendom disappears, those occasions may be lost forever, and I don't think that would be all to the good.

Finally I share the secular theologians' growing impatience with the plodding pace of church life. I get bored with the ranks of stolid burghers who make up so many of our congregations: good, clean Christian folk who want to be reassured that the world is in order and who see the Christian life in terms of conventional goodness. They have no sense of adventure, no passion (except when the minister changes the service or introduces a new hymn), no sense of being an *avant-garde*.

But we couldn't do without them. They pay the salaries of all us *avant-garde* types, permitting us to hold our *avant-garde*, antiburgher opinions in safety and comfort. And what is far more important, they also maintain the homes that produce good, honest, God-fearing kids that grow up to be wild and woolly *avant-garde* theologians. I just wonder if the church in the secular age will have the same capacity to produce this kind of sensitive and loyal criticism.

On the whole, I suppose I'm ready for secularization when it comes, though I'm not at all sure that it's really here yet. In America at least, the churches still seem strong and confident and generally in touch with most of the society. I don't hear many anticlerical social critics proclaiming with any confidence the imminent end of the Christian enterprise. And even the government has lately begun to call upon the churches to help carry out its own programs among the poor, the aged, and the illiterate. Maybe they're trying to tell us something.

But at the risk of being labeled a weak-kneed Israelite longing for the fleshpots of Egypt, I'd have to go further and say that though I'll live with secularization when it comes, I'm not going to do anything to help it along. Sufficient unto the day is the evil thereof. And it seems to me that we have enough trouble already without deliberately shaking our own foundations too much. All right, so I like it here in the bosom of Holy Mother Church, where it's warm and cozy. But I've been out in that secular world and believe me, it's cold outside!

Point of Order

OUR CULTURE is such an extraordinarly diverse phenomenon that almost anything can be said of it with
some plausibility. People are always describing for us
the characteristics of our age, our class, or our nation.
All such judgments contain a measure of truth, but they
become distorted when they are taken as the whole
truth. We have a tendency to accept the half-truth if it
is repeated often enough. The mass media serve to per-
petuate and to accentuate our misguided views about
ourselves.

Sociologists and anthropologists are more reliable
guides to the actual state of the culture, in spite of all the
nasty things that people say about them. The language of the craft, however, frequently makes the work

of the social scientist unavailable to the general reading public. Then, too, the social scientist must deal with averages, trends, and types. He cannot afford to deal with the atypical, the unique, the idiosyncratic.

Journalists can do better. Not the conventional newsman, of course, because he must always look for the sensation of the moment. I mean the solitary observer who can spot something out of the ordinary and can make some sense of it. Our better popular magazines sometimes serve this purpose, though they too get caught up in the conventional wisdom which is so often more conventional than wise. I have tried to serve as a journalist in this unconventional sense, using the insights of social scientists to present a theologically grounded picture of some aspects of our culture.

The theological perspective from which I view the culture stems from the conviction that the fundamental human sin is that of idolatry. Idolatry is the worship of false gods, the act of making absolute and primary that which is relative and contingent. In basic English, idolatry means taking the world too seriously.

In holding this view, I do not mean to downgrade the world's problems. I would only claim that since God alone is Lord, then despite all the negativities and contradictions of life and history, the universe is in safe hands. The theologian, like the ordinary believer, may have to hang onto his faith by his fingernails, but so long as he does hang on, he retains a certain deep-seated complacency about things. God, he is convinced, will survive. So will man—probably.